BRABHAM

FACING TITLE PAGE: A fine portrait of a grim-faced Jack Brabham ready for the 'off'; a picture taken just when aerofoils (see back of car) were coming into fashion.

BRABHAM

STORY OF A RACING TEAM

Phil Drackett

Arthur Barker Limited London
A subsidiary of Weidenfeld (Publishers) Limited

Published in Great Britain by
Arthur Barker Ltd
91 Clapham High Street
London SW4 7TA

ISBN 0 213 16915 0

Printed in Great Britain by
Butler & Tanner Ltd
Frome and London

CONTENTS

ACKNOWLEDGMENTS

'We will co-operate – to make sure you get it right.' So said Bernard Ecclestone, owner of the Brabham team, President of the Formula One Constructors' Association and arguably the most powerful man in motor racing today. For that co-operation and that of Gordon Murray, Nelson Piquet and other members of the present Brabham team, grateful thanks. My thanks also go to Sir Jack Brabham, who started it all, Christine McCaffrey, Sir Jack's personal assistant in the UK, Ron Tauranac and some of the many great drivers who have handled Brabham cars, notably Denny Hulme, Carlos Reutemann and the late Graham Hill.

Willing assistance has come from Anne Routledge, of Michelin, and photographers Michael Cooper and Nigel Snowdon; Lucia Rosati, S. Ghedini (Racing Department) and P. Boselli (Press Department) of Parmalat; Derek C. Guy of Castrol; Aert van der Goes (Racing Services Manager) of Koni BV (Holland) and Ashley Banks, of J.W.E. Banks, Koni's representatives in the UK; Robin Bradford (Press Officer) Brands Hatch circuit; and Ann Bradshaw (Press Officer) RAC Motor Sports Association.

Particular thanks to Neil Eason Gibson, racing enthusiast and son of a famous racing father, for assisting in the research, preparing the Appendixes and reading the final manuscript in a plane *en route* to Czechoslovakia; to Alan Brinton, companion in many a Press box who drew on thirty years of motor-racing memories; Dean Delamont, formerly Director of the RAC Motor Sports Association; and John Cooper, the man who gave Jack Brabham his big chance; all of whom gave freely and generously of their time.

Apart from those taken by Michael Cooper and Nigel Snowdon, the majority of the photographs are from the collections of J. van der Goes, Neil Eason Gibson and the author.

The author is also grateful to Martin Corteel, Sports Editor for the publishers and his predecessor Steve Dobell, together with Editorial Director, David Roberts, for their help and understanding; to Archie and Joyce Knowles; and to

Acknowledgments

'Beanball', otherwise my wife Joan, who has always been on hand to soothe the furrowed brow, supply endless cups of coffee and brightly produce the right word at the right time.

I hope we got it right, Mr Ecclestone. If we erred in any way then the fault is mine.

PHIL DRACKETT,
January 1985

FOREWORD

By Bernard Ecclestone

Since 1971 when I bought Motor Racing Developments Limited, which is the company that owns the Brabham Formula One Team, it has been my ambition to keep the name Brabham in the forefront of Formula One racing. This has been an extremely difficult task because a considerable amount of my time is taken up in my other capacity as the President of the Formula One Constructors' Association.

Although during the last years we have only managed to win two World Championships, we have done so using two different types of engine, firstly with the Cosworth 3 litre normally aspirated engine, and then with the BMW 1.5 litre turbo-charged engine, which was another first for Brabham because we were the first team to win a World Championship with a 1.5 turbo-charged engine. We would have had at least another World Championship had it not been for a rather unfortunate set of circumstances when Alan Jones took the title. We would have also won a lot more races had it not been for occasional mistakes on the team's part, or more often through circumstances beyond our control, but that is what racing is all about, and the reason people strive to do better.

I have been fortunate enough to have had in the company probably one of the best design engineers in the last decade, Gordon Murray. I have also been fortunate enough to have Nelson Piquet - that is during the last seven years - who is as much part of the Brabham family as Gordon and myself, and I am quite sure the team would not have held together in the friendly manner that it has if it had not been for the diplomatic way our team manager Herbie Blash carries out his job.

I hope that our team continues to partake in the same way that it has in the past, that is to say like a big family, and that we can notch-up another World Championship in 1985.

I am delighted that Phil Drackett has recorded the story of the team, and his book will be part of the Brabham history.

Chessington, Surrey
18 February 1985

Compared with today, motor racing in Australia was a bit primitive in Jack Brabham's salad days. Two Alfas and a twin-engine Special line up before the start of a race on an airfield circuit near Melbourne.

John Cooper, the man who set British motor racing on the right road and gave Jack Brabham his first big chance, seen in typically jovial mood with Jackie Stewart.

1
PROLOGUE

The thunder of a racing engine in full song echoed across the old airfield and faded into the green lanes surrounding it.

Only one of the Silverstone pits was occupied and a handful of mechanics peered out as a solitary car roared down the straight from Abbey Corner, into Woodcote and out past the stands to Copse Corner.

The driver felt happy ... the new tyres were handling well ... the car was hugging the road nicely ... he went smoothly through Becketts and down towards Stowe ... the rev. counter flickered as he accelerated out of Stowe and saw Club Corner looming up ahead ... the car was doing an effortless 113 mph ...

And then it happened. The car slewed across the track and at full tilt rammed the grassy bank on the corner, firmly imbedding itself in the earthy barricade.

The driver was still conscious but he could hardly move. The engine was revving wildly and it slowly dawned on him that his foot was jammed down on the accelerator. He tried gingerly to move his foot but something hard was pinned against it and the pain was excruciating.

He tried to reach the ignition switch, but trapped as he was it appeared out of his reach. In any event, as he took a second look at the instrument panel and saw how badly smashed it was, he doubted if any of the switches would work.

He looked around for help but there was none. There were no spectators, no marshals or officials and none of Silverstone's farm-workers in the vicinity. The pits and his own mechanics were away at the far end of the circuit, out of sight of Club Corner and the crashed car.

Then he relaxed. They would surely come out to look for him when he failed to come pass the pits on this lap. But would they? Not for a while anyway because it was not unknown for a driver when testing to stop out on the track somewhere to take a look at something which was bothering him. So it might be ten or fifteen minutes before they came out ...

Ten or fifteen minutes? With horror he realised that in a fraction of that time he and the car could be burnt to cinders.

The noise of a water-tap he could hear running was not in his imagination. Only it wasn't a water-tap. Fuel was running out of a split tank and with the engine still running, the whole shooting-match might go up in flames at any second . . .

He strained forward. His legs hurt like hell and now, as he tried once more to treach the instrument panel, the wreckage pressed across his chest felt like an iron band, restricting not only his movement but his breathing. But anything was preferable to burning alive . . .

With one violent effort he got close enough to the panel to hook a finger behind it. Sweating profusely, he desperately sought the correct wire, found it, wrenched hard. 'Thank God', the engine stopped.

He relaxed, but only for a moment. Stopping the engine had reduced the fire risk considerably but there was still a danger with all that fuel about that the heat would be enough to ignite it. And he was helplessly trapped in the cockpit.

The car had a built-in fire extinguisher and he prayed that it would work. He tried to think rationally. Should he activate the extinguisher now in a bid to prevent a fire starting? Or should he wait and see; using the extinguisher to put the blaze out if a fire did start?

The latter seemed the obvious course but he could foresee a snag. If the car did go up in flames the contents of the extinguisher might not be sufficient to quell the conflagration completely and there could be no escape. If that happened he was a dead man.

This made up his mind. He brought the extinguisher into play and as the life-saving foam surged out he prayed that it would keep fuel and hot metal apart until help reached him.

Eventually they came in search of him. They found him trapped, helpless . . . but alive and conscious. They had to cut him loose and when finally they lifted his big frame from the cockpit thirty minutes had elapsed since the car had rammed the bank with such terrifying force.

It was the longest thirty minutes of Jack Brabham's life. And if he had made the wrong decision that afternoon at Silverstone, most of this book could not, would not, have been written . . .

2

'BLACK JACK'

'I can't remember if it was the beginning of '54 or '55. I was on a round-the-world trip covering Canada, Australia and New Zealand, which was really the first post-war approach that motor sport enthusiasts in those countries had had from the RAC. The RAC was still officially the controlling body of all motor sport in the Commonwealth and the object of my tour was to set up independent organisations or delegate control to already existing organisations.

'It was at the New Zealand Grand Prix that one of the New Zealand officials, I think it was Ron Frost, who's still there, said he thought I'd be interested to meet a young Australian who was running his own car, a thing called the Redex Special, with which he'd won the Australian Championship. Actually it was a Cooper–Bristol of the same type that Mike Hawthorn used to drive.

'Some time about ten in the evening they took me along to a garage in Auckland and introduced me to this Aussie, by name, Jack Brabham.

'We got chatting and, in fact, were so busy chatting that I think the other people went off and we talked about his racing ambitions and would it be worthwhile coming to England and what opportunities were there and so on.

'As I recall we talked into the small hours of the morning and one way and another I think that clinched his decision to come to Europe.

'He came over a few months later and made a great mistake, I believe, by buying a Cooper–Alta which I think Peter Whitehead had raced. But that's another story...'

Thus said, in reminiscent mood, Dean Delamont, Competitions Manager and later Director of the RAC British Motor Sports Association, and thirty years on, still Jack Brabham's friend.

Brabham was known as 'Black Jack' in his native Australia. It could have been because of his jet-black hair, dark visage and chin-stubble, which refused to go away despite the best intentions of Messrs Gillette

13

Championship year: Jack Brabham (Cooper) in the 1960 Monaco Grand Prix, the year he won his second world title.

Jack Brabham in winning form at Silverstone in one of his own cars. Compare with Brabham's Cooper at Monaco to see how 'cigar tube' Grand Prix cars developed.

and Wilkinson & Co. The less liberally-minded opined that he was 'Black Jack' because of the ruthless way he cut a swathe through the primitive race circuits of post-war Aussie-land. Jack Brabham drove to win and his opponents were left in no doubt of that. But there was more to him than driving skill and determination because he was one of those drivers who knew and understood his car; a factor which gave him an edge over most of his rivals.

Dean Delamont again: 'I think Jack, like Graham Hill, was not so much a natural driver as many of them; but he was a brilliant engineer. It was the combination of his engineering skill and his driving skill which got him to the front. He was a very thoughtful driver. Someone once said that the art of being a successful racing driver was not to go faster than you had to and Jack had this ability.'

One adversary who knew as much about cars as Jack was Ron Tauranac, an expatriate Englishman who constructed his own cars, with the aid of his brother, and drove the family products exceedingly well. He and Jack had many a tussle and a mutual respect sprang up; a respect which was eventually to develop into a close partnership and the formation of the Brabham racing team.

Brabham was born in Sydney, Australia, on 2 April 1926, the son of a haulage contractor. After leaving school he trained as an automobile engineer, served in the Royal Australian Air Force, then opened his own garage.

He was twenty before he began his racing career in midget cars. It was there in the helter-skelter 'devil take the hindmost' atmosphere of the midgets that he was first talked of as a driver who could take care of himself. His progress was rapid and he was Australian Midget Car Champion four years in a row.

By the time a friendly New Zealander introduced him to Dean Delamont, Brabham was *the* Australian Champion, having proved himself in all sorts of racing. He was undeniably the best race-driver in the southern hemisphere and there were no fresh challenges to meet Down Under. His conversation with the RAC's motor-sport chief settled matters for him and in 1955 he arrived in the Old Country.

Brabham was not received with open arms by some of the Establishment – 'uncouth Colonial', one was heard to mutter – yet he did well in both sports cars and Formula Two single-seaters, coming to the attention of Charles Cooper and his son, John (then engaged in building a family garage-concern in Surbiton into the home of the dominant power in Grand Prix racing).

The little Cooper cars had dominated 500 cc and 1000 cc racing, the most popular form of the sport in the years immediately after the Second World War, father and son both driving cars of their own make.

John had scores of wins and places until the pressures of running the works team forced a gradual retirement. But a lad named Stirling Moss took up the running and driving a Cooper with a 996 cc JAP engine broke the Shelsley Walsh hill-climb record for unsupercharged cars, won the Lausanne Gold Cup and the Madgwick Cup, at Goodwood, in which he lapped at 84.7 mph, faster than any unsupercharged car under 3.5 litres had ever done.

Others who were to become famous Grand Prix drivers such as the Franco-American Harry Schell, Peter Collins and Ken Wharton, were cutting their racing eye-teeth on Coopers and so was a certain Bernie Ecclestone, who was to figure more significantly in the Grand Prix story than any of them.

Then came the Formula Two Cooper–Bristol, a winner in the hands of a young man named J.H. Hawthorn, better-known as 'Mike' and destined to be World Champion. From there it was a natural progression for the Coopers to turn their attention to Grand Prix racing. This then was the outfit which would give 'Black Jack' his big break.

Works and private entry Cooper drivers at the time included Roy Salvadori, Maurice Trintignant, Eric Brandon, Les Leston, Michael Christie, Ninian Sanderson, Bob Gerard, Alan Brown and Stuart Lewis-Evans, a roll-call of the famous in the first post-war decade. But the Coopers, stouthearted, good-natured, friendly men, yet astute judges of both cars and drivers, were always ready to encourage new talent.

Brabham, who after some misadventures with the Cooper–Alta had acquired a rear-engined Cooper–Bristol, was always hanging around the Cooper factory, asking for a 'works' drive. John Cooper, today President of the British Racing and Sports Car Club, recalls: 'I can see Jack now. He always seemed to be in overalls and carrying tools. And he would keep asking "When am I going to get a drive?"'

'One day Dad said to him, "I'm going to give you a works drive" – and he handed Jack the keys of the works transporter. Then Dad added, "And if you can get there without shunting it, you can drive one of the cars in the race." So that's how Jack became a Grand Prix driver.'

'Of course, he turned out one of the best. In my book, taking every-thing into consideration, the greatest. He was a damn good driver because he used his nut. Later when Bruce McLaren joined the team, what Bruce didn't know, Jack taught him. They were both good engineers. They could set up the cars and they didn't mind getting their hands dirty and working on them. I will always be terribly proud of the fact that the two of them went on to set up their own race-car manufacturing businesses and that both Brabham cars and McLaren cars were to win the World Championship.'

Vanwalls were the top British cars in 1957, the Coopers, fitted with Coventry–Climax engines, not having the power of their 2.5-litre rivals, but there were some grounds for optimism, Salvadori being second in the Caen Grand Prix while Brabham was fourth to two Connaughts and a BRM at Goodwood.

In 1958, the 32-year-old Australian picked up his first World Cham-pionship points – three of them – to be placed joint seventeenth with Cliff Allison, the Swede Jo Bonnier and the American Indianapolis star, Tony Bettenhausen, who did not race in Europe and gained his points solely in the 500. That was the year Mike Hawthorn took the title despite winning only one race to the four of Stirling Moss and three victories by Tony Brooks. At the time points were given for fastest laps and Hawthorn picked up five of these bonus points to Moss's three, edging his fellow Englishman out for the title by one point, 42 to 41. It was to be the nearest Moss ever came to the Championship and most people considered him desperately unlucky.

'That was the year we really began to think seriously of Cooper cars winning Grands Prix', says John Cooper, 'in fact cars entered by Rob Walker and driven by Stirling Moss and Maurice Trintignant had already done so. We had Roy Salvadori and Jack as "works" drivers and we felt with these two that our chances were pretty good.

'But BRM liked the look of Jack and they made an approach to him. I went to see Alfred Owen (Louis Stanley had made the approach) and Alfred said he would tell his team to "lay off" which he did.

'That wasn't the end of it, however. Reg Parnell was running the Aston-Martin Grand Prix team and he went after both Roy and Jack, offering them a lot more than we could pay. We couldn't expect the boys to turn down an attractive offer like that and we were pretty desperate. I went to Reg Tanner, Competitions' Manager of Esso (we were running on Esso at the time) and told him the situation. He was quite honest about it. He'd got some money to spare but not enough. He could bail us out with one driver but – "We can't afford both – which one do you want to keep?"

'At the time I would say that Roy was fractionally faster than Jack and I guess many people would have gone for him. But I had this feeling about Jack, the feeling that he had it in him to reach the top, and in the end this decided me to keep him and let Roy go. I think Roy was a bit surprised at the time.'

It was proved the right decision almost immediately. 1959 was Brabham's year... and Coopers', of course. He won only two races, the same as Moss and Brooks, but his consistent driving gave him the Championship by four points over Brooks. Five drivers in the top ten drove Coopers – Brabham, the young New Zealander Bruce McLaren, Moss, Trintignant and the American Masten Gregory.

This success sent Brabham winging home to Australia to talk to Ron Tauranac. His objective was to persuade Tauranac to come to Britain with him and join forces in building and running their own racing cars. (Tauranac, born in Gillingham, had left England as a 3-year-old.) Motor sport was booming and Jack was determined to be a part of it.

Tauranac listened, was convinced and booked his flight to England where he and Jack formed Motor Racing Developments Ltd. Meanwhile, Brabham rocketed to an even more convincing Championship success in 1960. He won five races (amongst the others, only Moss with two wins scored more than one) and took the title with a comfortable nine points margin over his team-mate, McLaren.

Bruce who, in time, was to emulate Jack and set up his own firm, was a model of consistency behind the wheel with one win and three second, two third and a fourth place. Coopers – with the first three drivers in the Championship handling their cars – were pretty happy too.

Years later, journalist Mike Kettlewell was to say: 'Jack Brabham was remarkable. No one really acknowledged it at the time but he was a truly great racing driver as well as a first-rate engineer. When he won the World Championship in 1959 and 1960 driving the "new-fangled" rear-engined Cooper, with its Climax engine, it was at a time when Stirling Moss was reputed to be the best driver. Headlines ran "Moss wins" or "Moss breaks down". Few noticed that Brabham was doing more winning and breaking down fewer times.'

Two great champions: Jack Brabham and Juan Manuel Fangio at Silverstone in 1963: standing behind Jack is John Eason Gibson, former race-driver who was for many years Silverstone's chief executive.

Brabham in 'show room' condition before the start of the 1963 Grand Prix of The Netherlands. Compare the tyre widths with those just five years later.

It is an opinion endorsed by Delamont. 'If you study Jack's career you find that he had very few crashes and even fewer serious ones. You *could* put that down to luck. I prefer to believe it was because he really knew what he was doing.'

Those who were not around motor racing at the time can have little idea of the heat generated by discussions on the merits of various Grand Prix drivers. In January, 1961, in my column in *Ford Times*, I was moved to write the following: 'When is a World Champion not a World Champion? When his name's Jack Brabham, apparently.

'No one has greater admiration for Stirling Moss and his prowess behind the wheel than this columnist but it seems I'm not the only one who is getting sick and tired of some of his admirers who think that they can best support their idol by denigrating Brabham. One of them even went so far as to write a letter to a distinguished contemporary which said, in effect, that Brabham was not entitled to call himself World Champion until he drove a BRM, or a Lotus, or some make of car other than a Cooper.

'Why the heck should he? The combination of Brabham and a Cooper has proved an irresistible one. I've always understood that in a motor race the object of the exercise is to win. Brabham and his Cooper do just that. Let's give him full credit for it. He's a likeable, pleasant personality, he came up the hard way, he backs sound driving methods with technical "know how". He is, in short, a worthy champion.

'The more fanatical supporters of Moss do their own hero a disservice. When Fangio was Champion, they said Moss was unlucky to be contemporary with such an exceptional driver; when Hawthorn won the title the scoring system was wrong. Now Brabham is king – and they call him lucky. This, mark you, for a man who won the 1960 title with the maximum number of points.

'Moss is brilliant. Brilliant enough to win the Championship. And maybe someday he will. Perhaps even this year.

'But his supporters should remember – there are other drivers.'

Sadly, Moss never did become Champion – a frightening crash at Goodwood finished his Grand Prix career, although he did later come back to other categories of motor racing.

Incidentally, from the same column, the *Autosport* annual rankings had Brabham and Moss as the only two five-star drivers, with Graham Hill, Phil Hill (USA), Innes Ireland and John Surtees as four-star men.

Given three stars were Tony Brooks, Jim Clark, Bruce McLaren, Jo Bonnier and Wolfgang von Trips. No Italians, no Frenchmen and only one German were in the top eleven.

A four-star and a three-star man, however, were to be the top drivers of 1961. A new 1.5-litre Formula was introduced to Grand Prix racing and the Italian Ferraris dominated the scene with the American Phil Hill and von Trips (surely the only German in history to be nicknamed 'Taffy'?) first and second in the title race.

Jack Brabham, with a meagre four points, was eleventh in the table. But he was not too depressed. In mid-season, the first car had emerged from the workshops of Motor Racing Developments, a Formula Junior single-seater. They called it the MRD.

Alan Brinton, a reporter who had forsaken the shrieks and noise of the Parliamentary Gallery for the shrieks and noise of the race track, protested vehemently at the name. 'They'll laugh at you on the Continent, Jack – it sounds like *merde* which means "shit" in French.'

'Pull the other one', said Jack, or words to that effect.

Alan takes up the story. 'Jack came back from a Continental trip and said, "Alan, you were right – we can't call the car MRD. What shall we do?" I said, "You'd better call them Brabhams" and so they have been to this day with the serial numbers beginning "BT", which stands for Brabham-Tauranac.'

That year marked the end of Brabham's association with the Cooper team. The first Brabham Grand Prix car, Coventry-Climax BT3 with a V-8 engine, was taking shape in the MRD workshops and Jack intended to drive it himself, having formed the Brabham Racing Organisation for the purpose. Meanwhile, until the BT3 was race-ready he purchased and used a Lotus 24.

The BT made its debut at the 1962 German Grand Prix, but it hardly caused a ripple on the Grand Prix scene in which BRM at last came into their own, Graham Hill taking the championship 12 points clear of Jim Clark (Lotus 25) and 15 points ahead of Brabham's erstwhile team-mate, Bruce McLaren (Cooper T60). Jack's combined efforts with the Lotus and the Brabham yielded him nine points and ninth position in the table. He was 36 and a lot of people thought him over the hill. They didn't know Jack.

Brabham wanted another driver. And he wanted a man who, like himself, had sound technical knowledge and a feel for engines. His eye lit upon Daniel Sexton Gurney, 6 ft 3 in., 182 lb., of tough American war veteran, a man who had seen service in Korea and had a playful little habit of forgetting his own strength and wrenching the gear-levers off cars.

Son of a New York opera singer, Gurney began his racing career in 1955 in sports car events in California. He started with a Triumph, graduated to a Porsche and then a husky 4.9-litre Ferrari. He came to Europe in 1958 to drive a 3-litre Ferrari at Le Mans and so impressed the Italian firm that he was signed as a 'works' driver the following year, making his Formula One debut in the French Grand Prix at Reims. In 1960, he moved on to the British BRM team and in 1961 and 1962 teamed up with Jo Bonnier in the German Porsche team, scoring his – and their – first Grand Prix win in the French Grand Prix at Rouen.

Gurney was persuaded to join Jack in a two-car team in 1963. Neither won a race but there was plenty of evidence that the Brabham Racing Organisation might yet be a force in the land. Driving the BT7, Gurney was again fifth in the championship with a second, third, fifth and sixth place. Jack, in a similar car, was seventh in the table with a second, fourth and fifth place. It was the year of the Lotus and Jim Clark – BRM and Graham Hill having to settle for runner-up.

Further progress was registered in 1964. Former world motor-cycling champion John Surtees, driving for Ferrari, now became king on four wheels as well, with Graham Hill (BRM) again runner-up and Clark (Lotus) relegated to third. Gurney and Brabham, still campaigning with BT7s, were sixth and eighth respectively, but Gurney broke the Brabham duck with wins in the French and Mexican Grands Prix.

The Brabham BT11 also made its appearance, another former motor-cyclist, Bob Anderson, scoring five championship points with a Climax-engined version whilst the Swiss driver, Jo Siffert, collected a couple of points more with a similar chassis powered with the 8-cylinder BRM56 engine.

It was Jim Clark's year again in 1965. The Lotus No. 1 took the World Championship, the Tasman Championship, the Indianapolis 500, the French and British Formula Two Championships and threw in some saloon-car races for good measure. A 'Grand Slam' of a kind rarely, if ever, seen before or since.

Gurney had a new Brabham, similar to Jack's, for the South African Grand Prix at East London but electrical troubles put him out on the fourth lap, whilst in the other works car, the Guv'nor had alternator trouble, came into the pits, and eventually finished eighth. Altogether there were six Brabhams in the sixteen cars classified at the finish, evidence that other entrants were convinced of the Brabham cars' merits. Siffert, entered in the Rob Walker Brabham–BRM, was seventh; Australian Paul Hawkins, in a Brabham–Ford entered by John Willment, ninth; another Aussie, Frank Gardner, in John Willment's Brabham–BRM, twelfth (Graham Hill had won the Rand GP, a non-Championship event, in this car a few weeks earlier); David Prophet (Brabham–Ford) fourteenth; and Bob Anderson (Brabham–Climax) sixteenth. The remaining Brabham driven by Jo Bonnier, retired on Lap 42.

Clark was the winner but he was absent for the next race at Monaco, taking part in the Indianapolis 500 instead. Gurney was also at 'Indy', his place in the Brabham team being taken by Denny Hulme. Lotus went missing altogether because the organisers refused to guarantee a place on the grid to their nominated drivers, Mike Spence (England) and Pedro Rodriguez (Mexico). The Rob Walker Brabhams of Bonnier and Siffert were there again, so was Bob Anderson and Willment had one car for Frank Gardner.

Jack shared the front row of the grid with Graham Hill. He took the lead from Bandini on Lap 34 but had to retire nine laps later when his oil pressure dropped. His rev. counter drive had failed much earlier but as he said, 'I could manage without a rev. counter but not without oil.' Meanwhile, Hill drove the race of his life to win at Monaco for the third year in a row. He was well in the lead by Lap 25 but at the chicane found Anderson's Brabham blocking the road. Hill went down the escape road and by the time he had pushed his car back on to the circuit, four of his rivals had gone by. But he broke the lap record time after time, was back in the lead by Lap 64 and stayed there to the end. Four Brabhams were amongst the ten cars classified with Hulme in eighth position.

Clark was back for the Belgium Grand Prix and scored his fourth successive victory in the race. Gurney was tenth – unhappy about the handling of his car in the wet – but Jack was a commendable fourth.

Gurney and Hulme had the works cars at Clermont-Ferrand, Jack deciding to give the New Zealander another run (he had won the Formula Two race at the same circuit the previous year). The American's 32-valve Climax gave trouble in practice and the Brabham mechanics replaced it with a 16-valve. Gurney ended up on the second row of the grid with Hulme on the third. Ironically, Gurney retired on Lap 17 with engine failure but Hulme stuck it out to the end and another fourth place. The winner was Clark, of course.

The Brabhams were out in full force for the British Grand Prix at Silverstone – three 'works' cars for Brabham, Gurney and Hulme; two Rob Walker entries for Bonnier and Siffert; John Willment's car for Frank Gardner and privateers Bob Anderson and Ian Raby.

One was a casualty at the start. Gurney's car, fitted overnight with a new Coventry-Climax engine, dropped a couple of valves on the warming-up lap and Dan hastily took over Jack's seat. A broken alternator belt put paid to Hulme on Lap 30 and gearbox trouble accounted for Anderson four laps later.

Clark (Lotus) and Hill (BRM) fought out a thrilling finish, the Scot winning by just 3.20 seconds. Gurney was a full lap behind in sixth place. The remaining Brabhams were seventh, eighth, ninth and eleventh of the thirteen cars classified as finishers.

Just two cars – for Gurney and Hulme – were entered for the Dutch race although the morale-supporting cast of Bonnier, Siffert, Gardner and Anderson was on parade. Clark won again – his fifth World Championship victory of the year and his third successive Dutch Grand Prix – with an up-and-coming young man named Jackie Stewart in second place. For Brabham, there was the consolation of third place for Dan Gurney after great tussles with Hill and Stewart. Hill finished fourth with Hulme in the other 'works' Brabham fifth. Gardner was eleventh and Siffert thirteenth.

The Nürburgring found Clark the winner again and the undisputed World Champion for 1965, but Hill, Gurney and Stewart all made a fight of it. Hill was second and Gurney again third as he had been at Zandvoort, separated from Brabham, 'the Guv'nor', by Jochen Rindt (Cooper–Climax). Bonnier drove one of Rob Walker's cars to seventh place.

The Italians made their usual all-out attack at Monza – four 'works' Ferraris, three BRMs entered by Scuderia Centro-Sud; and 'persuaded' Lotus to enter a third car for local driver, 'Geki', and Brabham one for Baghetti (Jack's own car).

In the sequel, fuel-pump trouble halted Clark's string of victories and Stewart won his first Grand Prix with team-mate Graham Hill second. Gurney was close behind them for another very creditable third place and Bonnier was seventh in the only other Brabham to finish. It left all the Italians 'crying into their spaghetti'.

Gurney and Jack himself drove the 'works' cars in the United States

Grand Prix; they were the only Brabhams entered, apart from Rob Walker's pair.

Proving the truth of the old adage that quality is better than quantity, Gurney and Jack drove impeccably to finish second and third, their best performance of the season. Alas, their Climax engines lacked the power of the BRM and Graham Hill won by some 12 seconds. Bonnier was eighth and Siffert eleventh.

So to Mexico City and the final Grand Prix of the year, with the same four drivers at the wheels of the same four Brabhams. Gurney, who started on the front row of the grid, drove a magnificent race, broke the lap record on Lap 57 but still had to give best to fellow American, Richie Ginther, who gave Honda their first Grand Prix win. Siffert was fourth in one of Rob Walker's cars but only eight finished. Jack went out on Lap 38 (oil) and Bonnier on Lap 43 with a metal fracture.

At the end of the day, Gurney had finished a plucky fourth in the Drivers' Championship and Brabham himself was tenth. Hulme, the other 'works' driver, was joint eleventh with Siffert.

Gurney and Brabham had come to the parting of the ways. The American wanted to move on since he too had plans to build his own cars. It was a time of change. With Coventry-Climax dropping out of racing and a new 3-litre formula coming in, engine changes were inevitable. On the other hand, Motor Racing Developments were extremely busy and many cars – Formula Two, Formula Three, Formula Junior and sports – were being sold to outside customers.

In fact, Brabhams were enjoying unparalleled success in forms of racing other than Grand Prix. The last year of Formula Junior – 1963 – had been dominated by the marque, with Gardner and Hulme the usual drivers. By 1965, Brabham dominated Formula Three. They also won the majority of 1964 Formula Two races and the Honda-engined models completely swept the board in 1966. (The association with Honda was to continue, as far as Jack was concerned, to the present day.) In 1965, Hulme sensationally won the Tourist Trophy, the world's oldest surviving auto race, in a BT8 sports car with Coventry-Climax engine of only 2 litres. Production of all types of Brabham racing car had passed the 300 mark by 1967. It is interesting to note that some 17 years later, a Brabham BT23 (chassis number BT23/1), an ex-works Formula Two car, was being offered for sale at £7,000. However, nothing could disguise the fact that, in the end, it was Grand Prix racing that mattered.

Front row of the grid for
International Trophy at
Silverstone, 1964. Dan
Gurney and Jack Brabham
in the 'works' Brabhams are
No's. 5 and 6. Graham Hill,
later to join the Brabham
team, is in car No. 3.

Jack summed-up the situation at the end of the 1965 season: 'Our team figured fairly consistently in the results – Dan got a couple of second places and three thirds – but victory eluded us. I didn't take part in all the Grands Prix which led some people to suggest that I was getting ready to retire from the cockpit. Frankly, there *were* times when I felt like hanging up my helmet because we seemed to be working like blazes for too little return. But one thing kept me going and gave me heart.'

What that 'thing' was, we shall find out.

Alan Brinton again: 'Jack plays everything close to his chest. I believe that during his career as a driver and as a manufacturer I was the journalist closest to him yet there was much he didn't tell me.

'When there was a big question mark on how and where Brabham would get suitable engines for 1966, Jack just grinned at me and said, "Yeah, it's a right old state of affairs and no mistake." And all the time he knew he had solved the problem.'

Jack explains: 'I'd been doing my best to keep all my rivals guessing by hinting that it would be impossible to continue Grand Prix racing if I didn't have an engine. Well, it was true, wasn't it?'

But he did have an engine.

Back in Melbourne, Australia, Repco, 'the biggest manufacturer of automotive parts and service equipment in the southern hemisphere and exporters to 85 countries', were building an engine developed by Jack's partner, Ron Tauranac. It was built around the Oldsmobile F85 V8 block and was a simple affair with only a single overhead camshaft to each bank of cylinders.

The other teams were going in for *power* in a big way. BRM had a complicated and highly-sophisticated 16-cylinder; Ferrari a V12, based on an already race-proven design; Coopers were preparing to use a Maserati V12; Honda were working on a 12-cylinder job; and Gurney's Eagles were also to have V12s. To illustrate the difference between the Brabham engine and the others, Honda would start the Mexico race with 52 gallons aboard; Brabham with 28. Brabham also retained a small-diameter tubular steel space-frame at a time when others were following the monocoque fashion set by Lotus.

Jack started the new season in a BT19, a chassis originally built in 1965 to take a 16-cylinder Coventry-Climax engine which, of course, never arrived. Now the back end was sliced off and the car adapted for the Repco 620 engine.

Brabhams were running on Goodyear tyres. The Akron, Ohio, firm did not build racing tyres until 1958 and it was not until 1965 that they got into Formula One, their first teams being Honda and Brabham.

Richie Ginther's winning drive for Honda in Mexico that year gave them their first Grand Prix victory – 'Black Jack' was to do even better by them.

Jack laconically and grudgingly admitted that he might, just might, pick up a win or two at a the start of the season whilst the more sophisticated machinery was getting over its teething problems. 'In private, having seen what some of the others were getting up to, I thought I could do better than this.'

As it turned out, Jack stuck to what he called his '1965½' car, or his 'old nail', for most of the 1966 season, apart from the last couple of races. The 'proper' 3-litre car, the BT20, was driven throughout by Denny Hulme. The two BT11s were still on the trail, Bob Anderson with the Climax version and John Taylor with the BRM.

After breakdowns in the non-Championship South African Grand Prix and Syracuse Grand Prix, Jack gave a taste of what was to come by leading from start to finish in the Silverstone International Trophy – also non-Championship – and setting a new Formula One lap record in the process.

The team set off for Monte Carlo in high spirits. It was there in 1959 that Jack had gained his first win in a Championship race, a win which set him off on the road to his first world title. Now they hoped that history might repeat itself.

It was not to be. The Brabham transporter was delayed on the road and they missed the first practice session. Then the new engine fitted to Jack's car would not run properly and had to be replaced by the 'Silverstone' engine.

As if that wasn't enough, Jack woke up on race morning with 'the dreaded lurgi'. He had a miserable drive and felt so rotten that he was almost relieved when his gearbox packed up on the seventeenth lap. 'I watched the race for a few laps, caught a bus back to my hotel along the coast and was in bed long before Jackie Stewart was acclaimed the winner.'

The next round was at Spa-Francorchamps. The cars set off in the dry and then ran into a wall of water after only two miles. Seven out of the fifteen starters were through with the race in the first minutes. Brabham himself lost control at 135 mph, headed straight for a house, slid sideways and came to a halt just short of some straw bales.

Life was getting serious. Jack hadn't won a Grand Prix himself since 1960, the year of his second World Championship, and his cars hadn't done very much better in other hands. The luck was about to change...

At Reims, with its long fast straights, the Brabhams were figured to be outgunned by the Ferraris and Coopers. It didn't quite work out like that. The Coopers had a lot of trouble and as Jack said: 'I managed to cling on to Lorenzo Bandini's Ferrari at the start and got a valuable tow from his slip-stream. The straights at Reims were long and real power mattered there. While I could keep in the Ferrari's slip-stream I was touching 182 mph down the fastest straight. After Bandini got away and I was on my own, my top speed dropped to only 174 mph.

'Bandini got well into the lead but had his throttle-cable snap. This let me into a very comfortable lead over Mike Parkes in the other Ferrari and after that I just had to concentrate on cruising home.'

Thus Jack Brabham became the first driver in the history of Grand Prix racing to win one of the classics in a car of his own manufacture. He owed some thanks to the misbegotten Italian mechanic who forgot to fit a stop to Bandini's throttle pedal, but he would never have been in a position to take advantage of that error had he not had the wit to cling on to Bandini from the start. As Dean Delamont says, 'A thoughtful driver, our Jack.'

The next race was at Brands Hatch to which twisty circuit the Brabham cars were ideally suited and Jack proceeded to set fastest lap with team-mate Hulme second fastest. The pair were never under pressure in the race itself and finished one and two respectively.

Before the Dutch Grand Prix, Brabham, now 40 but fed-up with scribes who called him 'the old man of motor racing', hobbled up to the grid wearing a long, false beard, an unusual leg-pulling gesture from a man who appeared somewhat serious in mien to the world at large.

A lot of oil was dropped on the circuit and Jim Clark took his chances to pass Brabham at about one-third distance, increasing his lead to 10 seconds when Jack was hampered in passing slower cars. Brabham kept up the pressure, however, and eventually re-passed Clark. A couple of pit-stops dropped Clark to third at the finish and Brabham motored comfortably home a lap ahead of Graham Hill (BRM).

The German Grand Prix at the Nürburgring made it four in a row for

Jack Brabham in another guise – flagging away the starters in the RAC International Rally of Great Britain. On the right is RAC Motor Sports Director Dean Delamont, the man who convinced Jack his racing future was in Europe.

Jack Brabham is presented with a specially-struck gold medal to commemorate winning both the World Drivers' and World Manufacturers' Championships in 1966. Centre is Howard Mathias, RAC Vice-Chairman, and right The Marquis Camden, Chairman of the RAC Competitions Committee.

Jack despite a tremendous challenge from John Surtees (Cooper–Maserati) and meant that only Surtees and Jackie Stewart had an outside chance of catching Jack for the Championship.

All three retired at Monza, which was a Ferrari benefit with Scarfiotti first and Parkes second. Thus Jack Brabham won the World Championship for the third time, the first driver to win the title in a car of his own manufacture, sitting on a pit counter at Monza and watching the rest of the Grand Prix circus go by. Then he gave himself a congratulatory pat on the back by winning the non-Championship Gold Cup at Oulton Park.

Although the struggle for the driver's laurels was resolved, there remained the Constructors' Championship. This was still in the balance since Ferrari were in with a chance if they could win the US Grand Prix at Watkins Glen with the Mexican Grand Prix still to come. Brabham again retired but so did Ferrari's Bandini and the Constructors' Cup joined the Drivers' on the Brabham mantelpiece. Officially, of course, it went to Motor Racing Developments (Ron Tauranac and Jack Brabham) – with a little aid from Girling brakes, Esso fuel, Lucas equipment, Superseal oil pumps and water seals and Goodyear tyres.

The season ended with a second place in the Mexican Grand Prix, but it was all academic by then.

Of all the Brabham supporters, Goodyear were probably the happiest. Brabham had brought them their *first* World Championship, quite something for a firm which had been founded as long ago as 1898. There was an added bonus for the American tyre firm as Brabham also took the Formula Two Championship.

Goodyear's technical mastery launched a new tyre 'war', intensified when Denny Hulme repeated the Brabham success in 1967. Development work went on at a pace not seen before and one result was a startling increase in the width of tyres.

In 1965 Goodyear had been using tyres with a tread width of 5 inches. By the end of that year, the width was 6 inches and Jack's Championship year of 1966 saw $7\frac{1}{2}$ inches as the normal equipment. In 1967 10-inch tyres were introduced and at the beginning of 1968 Goodyear brought out $11\frac{1}{2}$-inch tyres for their contracted teams of Brabham, McLaren and Gurney. By the middle of the season, Gurney was running tyres with a tread $13\frac{1}{2}$ inches wide and they were to get wider yet . . .

In 1970, a totally treadless tyre (an innovation taken from drag-racing) was tried on a Formula One car and from the beginning of the 1971 season all dry-weather tyres took the form of these 'slicks' as. they were known, treads being retained for the wet weather. Another drag-racing innovation was also used in Formula One that year – soft 'wrinklewalls' which wound up like a spring in slow corners then literally catapulted the car out of the corner.

Modest Jack summed-up: 'None of it would have been possible without the devoted work of all my team to whom I cannot give enough credit. You know, actually driving the car in the races is – at least for me – only a minor part of the effort. The major effort goes on behind the scenes in preparing and developing the cars so that they are fast and reliable when the flag falls. Repco provided me with the power I needed and the Australian-built engine confounded the prophets in no uncertain manner. And really, you know, the way the forecasters were wrong was for me a lot of the fun.'

Jack's loyalty to 'his team' was repaid by their loyalty to him. Australian-born mechanic Tim Wall was with Jack for six years from the time of Jack's first title win for Cooper until he left the Brabham team when Dan Gurney quit to build his own car, the Eagle, and offered Tim the Chief Mechanic's job, a challenge Tim could not refuse. Wall saw some great days in motor racing including two years with Stirling Moss in the Rob Walker 'private' Cooper team during which Moss won the 1958 Argentine Grand Prix against the might of Ferrari and Maserati.

The Brabham mechanics the year Jack won the title with his own car, all Australians or New Zealanders, were Chief Mechanic Roy Billington who, with Hughie Absalom and Gary Taylor, worked on Jack's car; John Muller, in charge of Denny Hulme's car; and Bob Ilich, the engine specialist. And, of course, both Brabham and Hulme were mechanics themselves and knew what it was all about.

Billington, famed for his ability to cat-nap in the transporter *en route* to the circuit no matter how bumpy or dusty the road, had a philosophy of racing much the same as that of his boss: 'The satisfaction is not in winning but in the car staying together, proving that the job of preparation had been well done.'

There were some who thought our Jack too self-effacing. Big David Phipps, editor, writer and photographer, one of that small élite band who follow the Grand Prix circus around the world, commented. 'One of the oldest adages of motor racing concerns the expediency of winning at the *lowest* possible speed. One of the most difficult facets of motor racing is to slow down without losing concentration. Jack Brabham was a master in both respects.'

3

HULME AS IN HULL'M

Denny Hulme, a craggy-faced man looking much older than his years, came from the right stock. Born in Te Puke, New Zealand, on 18 June 1936, he was the son of Clive Hulme, who was to be awarded the Victoria Cross in the Second World War. The family pronounce their name 'Hull'm' and not in the English fashion of 'Hume'. Father Clive always said, 'You can't knock the "L" out of "Hulme".'

Denny graduated into the Brabham 'works' team the hard way, working at the factory as a mechanic when he was not driving Formula Junior cars. Early on he was nicknamed 'The Bear', allegedly by pressmen who complained that he wasn't always ready to be interviewed or deliver smiles to order for the benefit of their cameras. But other folk thought he looked like an amiable grizzly.

When Denny helped Jody Scheckter, the South African driver, at the outset of *his* Grand Prix career and the two were often seen together, Scheckter inevitably became known as 'Little Bear'.

Hulme, after an illustrious career with the Brabham team, was to leave them and join McLaren in 1968. This was understandable in many ways since Bruce, a quiet pleasant man, was in so many respects another Jack Brabham. And after all Bruce *was* a fellow New Zealander . . .

That first McLaren season of 1968, Hulme won the Can–Am Championship, a feat he repeated two years later. He retired from racing in 1974 and now lives in his native New Zealand. According to a friend, he misses the racing scene very much.

Denny first attracted attention by winning the 1960 Vic Hudson Memorial Trophy at Levin in a 2-litre Cooper-Climax, a success which prompted the New Zealand International Grand Prix Association to send him to Britain under their 'Driver for Europe' scheme – with the fare and living expenses paid for a year.

Hulme was, in fact, another Cooper graduate. An analysis of the top racing-drivers over a period of 20 years after the Second World War reveals an amazing number of them who first tasted victory at the wheel of a Cooper. But when Denny first came to the UK it was to a tough hard world with plenty of competition and many adversaries who were not in the least impressed by anyone being selected as New Zealand's top driver.

There was no overnight success. Indeed, Denny ended up working at Jack Brabham Motors, carrying out conversions on Alpines and Rapiers and hoping for a drive in the Brabham Formula Junior car. That chance came at Crystal Palace, when Hulme set fastest practice time and was fourth in the race. Then on Boxing Day, 1962, he was again given a drive and this time he won. It prompted Brabham to give him a contract for 1963, although he would have to wait two more years for a Grand Prix seat. But the wait would be worthwhile . . .

It was on a hot Sunday afternoon in October, 1967, that Jim Clark won the Mexican Grand Prix in his Lotus 49, with Jack Brabham second and Denny Hulme third. But the rugged New Zealander was the happiest of the three because that third place was sufficient to gain him the World Championship, whilst Jack's disappointment at not gaining the title for the fourth time was more than tempered by the fact that the champion driver was again in a Brabham car.

Coming up to that final race of the season, the two Brabham drivers were the only real contenders for the title, but whereas Jack had to win with Hulme no better than fifth to take the honours, Denny had only to ensure that he kept one place behind his boss to be the victor.

Hulme commented: 'Though our cars carried the same colours we were both determined to take that coveted title if we could and once we set off for the grid it was each for himself.

'All the same, it was a curious situation, because remember I was driving a car belonging to Jack and prepared by his mechanics: the fact that the car ran faultlessly throughout is a fine tribute to the fair way everyone played this tense game.'

Clark was the pre-race favourite but in practice Chris Amon (Ferrari), Dan Gurney (Eagle-Weslake) and Graham Hill (Lotus 49) were also faster than the two Brabhams, which started side by side on the third row of the grid, more of a handicap to Jack than his team-mate.

Hulme takes up the story. 'Well, the race went exactly as I planned, I didn't exactly pussyfoot it but I concentrated hard on keeping my car in one piece. My engine was given a rev. limit of between 8,300 and

8,400 rpm but as an insurance against breakdown I never went above 7,500 rpm throughout the whole race. But this was enough to keep station behind Jack who had a rough old time of it that day with above-normal oil temperatures. He had to work very hard indeed to finish second to Jim.'

One of Hulme's satisfactions in taking the title was that he felt he had finally justified the faith put in him by the New Zealand Grand Prix Association when they paid for him to come to Europe back in 1960.

The season had opened at Kyalami with the South African Grand Prix. The two Brabhams were one and two on the grid and one and two in the race until Jack had overheating trouble. Hulme, yet to win a Grand Prix, took a comfortable lead – until three-quarters distance when his brakes went sick. He made a couple of pit-stops but the trouble couldn't be cured and he carried on 'without anchors'. 'It was by no means a funny situation,' Hulme recounted, 'rushing down the straight at over 160 miles per hour and trying to slow down by slipping down through the gears. Luckily I managed to stay on the road and finish the race – but only in fourth place. It was a terrifying ride.' Of course, it was a ride which many drivers would never have attempted. Denny Hulme was truly a chip off the old block.

At Monaco – Jack Brabham's lucky track – Hulme finally gained a win. 'My victory was due in part to oil laid down by other cars and particularly by Jack, who had a big blow-up on the very first lap. My car was handling so well that I was able to press on harder on the oil-soaked circuit than most of the others. There was one lap where I got a bit tweaked coming out of the chicane and had a brush with the straw bales on the quay but mercifully the car got itself straight again. I also touched the guard-rails at Tabac Corner and ran over the pavement at the Hôtel de Paris but the Repco-Brabham was tough enough to take punishment and it was a fine feeling to take that chequered flag.'

Nothing succeeds like success. That same month Denny finished fourth at Indianapolis and was named 'Rookie of the Year' at the great American classic.

At Zandvoort for the Dutch Grand Prix, the new Lotus 49 with Ford V8 engine, designed by Keith Duckworth, made its debut and Jim Clark showed the Brabhams a clean pair of rear tyres.

Clark was only sixth in the Belgian race but it wasn't much help to Jack and Denny, both Brabhams retiring with oil-surge problems. Clark

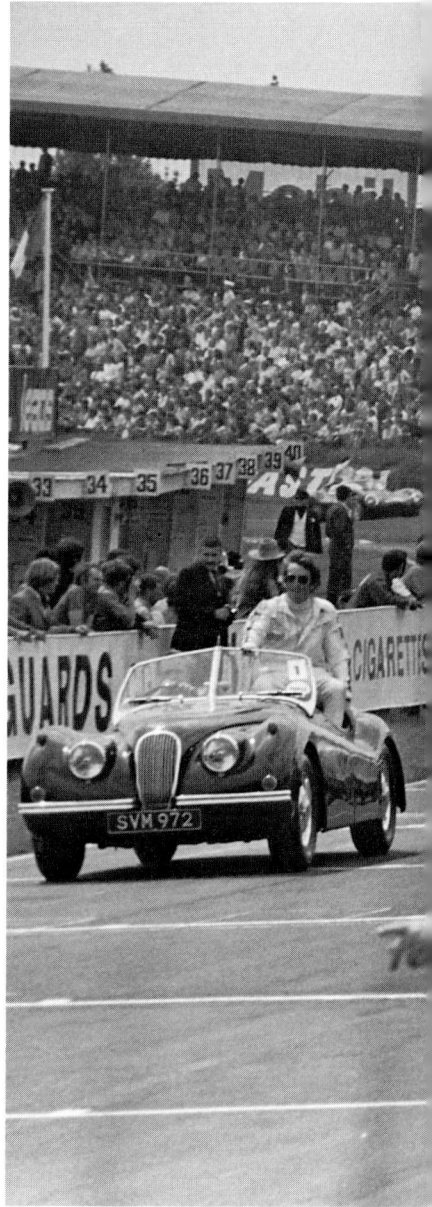

Jack Brabham is congratulated by the Chairman of the RAC, Wilfrid Andrews, at a dinner in the RAC Clubhouse, after Jack had won the World Championship for the first time.

Drivers parade the circuit in a fleet of Jaguars: Jack Brabham is in car No. 2, Denny Hulme in No. 3, just behind. The man directing traffic in the foreground is Michael Southcombe, later to become Chairman of the RAC Motor Sports Association.

was the winner again at Silverstone, but this time Hulme managed second place, ahead of Amon (Ferrari).

The French Grand Prix that year was staged on the twisty little Bugatti circuit at Le Mans with its constant gear-changes. Hulme lost the knob of his gear-lever on the third lap and had to change thereafter with the short, bare rod. He was very relieved when the race was over and he could get some treatment for his bruised and blistered hand. The Lotuses failed this time and Jack Brabham won with the gallant Hulme second.

In Germany at the Nürburgring it was Hulme's turn to win with Jack second and in the Canadian Grand Prix at Mosport, Jack was the winner. Denny did well to finish second after spinning-off in the rain. The engine stopped but, fortunately, it re-started immediately on the button – something Grand Prix engines don't always do – and Hulme got away again without any trouble.

In the Italian Grand Prix, Hulme had problems with a head-gasket in practice and a repeat of this in the race itself forced him into retirement before halfway. Jack nearly won, being pipped by John Surtees by what was officially given as one fifth of a second.

The United States Grand Prix at Watkins Glen was important in many ways. Clark and Hill were first and second and Brabham, who lost three laps through a puncture, was fifth. Hulme was third and these two places over Brabham were to prove decisive in Mexico.

Said Denny: 'Again I had to thank Jack. You see, after he had his puncture they slowed me down because they feared my tyres might be wearing too rapidly. If I hadn't been slowed it is extremely unlikely that I would have finished because I ran out of petrol on the last lap and just coasted across the line with a dead engine. But for that SLOW pit signal I could have run out of petrol much earlier and would not have even secured third place.'

There was further reason for joy in the Brabham camp because for the second year in succession they had won the Constructors' Championship.

With the season ending on such a bright note, Jack and Ron Tauranac could have been forgiven if they looked forward to further success in 1968. But motor racing is the most unpredictable of all unpredictable sports.

The first blow was the loss of 'The Bear' who took his World Championship to the McLaren camp. McLaren was doing what Brabham and Gurney had done before him, running his own team, and to a fellow New Zealander it must have been an attractive proposition.

The Brabham camp was not too worried about the defection because there was a replacement to hand. Jochen Rindt, usually described as an Austrian, was in fact born in Germany of a German father and Austrian mother. Both his parents were killed in an air-raid in 1943 and young Jochen was taken care of by his maternal grandparents who lived in Gratz, Austria.

Rindt started in motor sport in rallies and saloon car races and, at the age of 21, turned to single-seaters with a Formula Junior Cooper in 1963. He won a Formula Two race at Crystal Palace the following year, was offered a Formula One drive by Rob Walker and ended up with a three-year contract with Cooper-Maserati. He won Le Mans in 1965 and was tipped by many as a coming World Champion. If anyone could replace Hulme, Rindt looked like the man.

Joining the team at the same time was a Cooper mechanic named Ron Dennis. He was eventually to become the owner of the McLaren team and said he got the idea after being handed the management and finances of the Brabham team between the United States Grand Prix and the Mexican Grand Prix. 'I thought if I can do this sort of thing for someone else, why can't I do it for myself?'

Dennis answered his own question by eventually taking over a McLaren team which had Niki Lauda and Alain Prost vying for the World Championship with the rest nowhere.

The Repco-engined Brabham had proved itself stronger and more reliable than the new Ford-engined Lotus 49, although not so fast. So Ron Tauranac produced a better car, the BT26 and Repco produced a 'better' engine, the 2996 cc Repco 860, a twin-cam eight-cylinder unit. It looked like another winning formula but, alas, there was a weak link which was soon to make itself apparent.

The first Grand Prix of the 1968 season proved nothing very much, one way or the other. South Africa was a resounding win for Lotus, Clark and Hill finishing first and second, but Rindt was only seconds behind Hill to take third place. Unfortunately for the future of the Brabham *equipe*, Rindt was driving a car powered by the *old* engine.

Terrible tragedies were ahead for Lotus. Mike Spence, their No. 3 driver, was killed in practice for the Indianapolis 500 Mile Race; and Jim Clark, No. 1, in a Formula Two race at Hockenheim, a fatality which shook not only the racing world but was the subject of front-page headlines everywhere.

The 'works'. Brabham at the 1968 Dutch Grand Prix. The wide
Goodyears make the entire car look bulkier – and deadlier.

Jack Brabham discusses a problem with one of his mechanics prior to the
1969 Dutch Grand Prix.

Brabham racing cars were sold all over the world. Here Greg Cusack in
the Scuderia Veloce Brabham Repco V8 is on his way to victory in the
1967 Sydney Motor Show Trophy at Warwick Farm.

Graham Hill, No. 2, was to respond to the challenge and win the Drivers' Championship, at the same time helping Lotus to win the Constructors' Championship. But that was to come . . .

Meanwhile, the Brabham team had found out just what was wrong with their plan to win the Championship again. It was the new engine. It proved terribly unreliable and Spain, Monaco, Belgium, Holland, France and Brands Hatch went by before Rindt scored another third place, this time at the Nürburgring, with Jack Brabham fifth. It was the only race the pair were to finish for the rest of the season, Canada, USA and Mexico all being non-productive.

It was a severe blow to Rindt's title aspirations. Twelfth in the Championship, with a meagre eight points, he must have wondered what he had got himself into. As for the Guv'nor, the three-times World Champion found himself twenty-third, joint bottom of the table with Silvio Moser, in a private Brabham, at two points apiece. And the Brabham team was a lowly eighth in the Constructors' Championship.

This was also the year of the aerofoils when cars began to sprout all sorts of wing-like appendages in a bid to hug the ground more closely and go faster. The purists were aghast – what was the Grand Prix world coming to? – but Graham Hill, his Brabham days in the autumn of his career yet to come, said, 'A great deal of nonsense has been said and written about this innovation, most of it as far as I can see, by people who have never driven a racing car so fitted. All I can say is that a car with an aerofoil is very nice to drive and – which is the object of the exercise – faster on most circuits with the possible exception of Monza. Just another case where, if you read some of the "experts", you wonder how you have been passing your time.'

Rindt could hardly be blamed for looking elsewhere for 1969 and he did not have far to look. Lotus had the top car but had lost the top driver, Clark. Rindt was the obvious replacement.

The Brabham team had more to worry about than the loss of Rindt. The Repco power-plant was obviously not up to the task so Brabham faced the inevitable and joined the long list of Ford–Cosworth users.

It was a decision not lightly taken. Jack thought very seriously about giving up Grand Prix racing but the indomitable Aussie spirit came to the fore, 'After all, it wouldn't have looked very good to bow out at the end of such a disastrous year.' Jack made his decision rather late so the 'new' Brabham which Ron Tauranac produced for 1969 was a modified 1968 design, the BT26A.

Filling Rindt's empty cockpit wasn't easy either but finally they secured the very good young Belgian driver, Jacky Ickx. Son of one of the most famous of motoring journalists, Jacques Ickx, Jacky was born in Brussels in 1945. Motor cycling was his first love and he was three-times Belgian Trials Champion before turning to hill-climbs and racing. Ken Tyrrell signed him for Formula Three in 1966 and the following year he won the European Formula Two Championship. He made his Grand Prix debut in 1967 when he replaced the injured Mexican, Pedro Rodriguez, in the Cooper team and came to Brabham after a year under contract to Ferrari. Later he was to win Le Mans so many times that the wags joked that he owned the place. He also became Clerk of the Course at Monaco.

Testing the first Brabham–Ford BT26A at Goodwood before shipping out for the South African Grand Prix, Jack felt his luck was about to change, an opinion confirmed when he got the pole position at Kyalami. At the time Grand Prix cars were wearing wings which, like little Topsy, seemed to grow and grow and Jack – prematurely as it turned out – attributed his pole time to Brabham having the best wings in the business. Ironically, in the race itself both he and Ickx were forced to retire because of wing breakage.

A sounder reason for the fast time was the tyre situation, the team having done its testing at Kyalami. Unfortunately, the same tyres didn't suit Barcelona, Monaco and Zandvoort and the only early-season win was a non-Championship victory at Silverstone in March; Goodyear redeeming themselves with a wet-weather tyre which enabled Jack to lead the *Daily Express* Trophy from start to finish. However, it was a close-run thing. Jack started the last lap $9\frac{1}{2}$ seconds ahead of Rindt's Lotus, but ran out of fuel on the last corner and just managed to roll across the line with a dead engine – a little over two seconds in front of the Lotus driver. Ickx, in the other 'works' Brabham, was fourth.

At Barcelona, the team had tyre problems, Jack had engine trouble and Ickx did well to finish sixth after his rear-wing broke. Repairs to Jack's engine cost £2,400 which may not sound a lot by 1985 standards but was a 'helluva' lot of money then.

Ickx was battling with Piers Courage for second place at Monaco when his rear suspension broke. Jack, meantime, had a remarkable coming together with the BRM of John Surtees. The latter had sudden gearbox

Jochen Rindt, former Brabham 'works' driver, was the only man to be posthumously awarded the World Title. He was killed in practice for the 1970 Italian Grand Prix but had an unassailable points lead.

Jack Brabham, leading the 1970 British Grand Prix, ran out of fuel a few hundred yards from the line, enabling Jochen Rindt to win. Exhausted with his efforts to get the car over the line, a bewildered and bemused Jack was stopped by officials from breaking the finish-line beam – on foot.

trouble and, thinking Jack was behind him, pulled over to let him through. Unfortunately, by that time Jack was almost alongside him. The resulting collision took off one of Jack's rear wheels as clean as a whistle and he went through the tunnel with three wheels and no brakes. Emerging into daylight at the other end of the tunnel there was only one way to stop the car and he had to run it into the wall, fortunately without too much damage to man or machine.

The Dutch Grand Prix was a little better. Both cars were troublesome from time to time but in spite of that Ickx managed fifth place with Jack behind him in sixth.

The French Grand Prix was next and Jack fancied the Brabham chances on the fine circuit at Clermont Ferrand. Especially as the team was promised some improved tyres.

Brabham went to Silverstone to test the new tyres – and missed the next three Championship races. The reason was the frightening crash described in the prologue to this book . . .

Jack emerged from the crash with a broken left ankle which had to be screwed together, sidelining him until the Italian Grand Prix in September.

Jack couldn't even be a spectator at the French Grand Prix where Jacky Ickx just lost second place to Jean-Pierre Beltoise (Matra) on the last lap. The Belgian went one better at Silverstone where he *did* finish second. It was almost a repeat of the *Daily Express* race. Ickx's engine stopped on the last lap and, thinking he had run out of fuel, Jacky didn't try to re-start it. Instead he coasted to the line and was nearly caught by Bruce McLaren. Jack did see this heart-stopper – Ford loaned him an automatic transmission Zodiac for personal transport.

Third, second – and at Nürburgring – there was finally a victory. Ickx estimated that he had driven 10,000 miles at the 'Ring with its 170 corners and it paid off as he showed by his domination of the race. It was a great moment for Jack himself. It had been nearly two years since a Brabham car had won a major classic – the Canadian Grand Prix at Mosport in 1967 – 'My only regret was that we had a second car sitting in the paddock with nobody to drive it.'

The only good thing about the Italian race which followed was that Jack's ankle was sufficiently recovered for him to drive. Everything else about the race was a disaster. The team blew up two engines practising in England and two more in official practice at Monza, having to borrow one from Frank Williams so that Ickx could start the race. The race itself was no better, neither car finishing. It was a disappointment after the Ring, a painful disappointment since the least-damaged of the four wrecked engines cost £800 to repair.

Another engine went in practice for the Canadian Grand Prix and a second went sick on race morning. The Brabham mechanics replaced both in about two hours apiece and Ickx got his second win of the season with the Guv'nor just behind him. A win with more than usual satisfaction for the 'backroom boys'.

Ickx was now in with an outside chance of the Drivers' Championship, led by Jackie Stewart, but in the United States Grand Prix he suffered engine failure at three-quarters distance. Jack Brabham finished fourth, after a race in which for much of the time both Brabhams were engaged in a tremendous contest with Piers Courage, driving a BT26. Jack must have had mixed feelings when the numerous Brabham customers started giving the 'works' cars a tough time.

At the final round in Mexico, Jack was in pole position with Ickx on the front row beside him. Jack's car had some off moments while Ickx found himself affected by the heat. Both recovered sufficiently for Jack to finish third and Ickx second, the winner being former Brabham 'works' driver Denny Hulme.

It hadn't been a bad season after all – two wins, three seconds, two thirds and a fistful of minor places. Ickx was runner-up for the Drivers' Championship and the marque was second for the manufacturers' award.

It was enough to persuade Jack to continue in Grand Prix racing in 1970 and Ron Tauranac produced the first monocoque Brabham Formula One car, the BT33. Jack won first time out with it – in South Africa – but for the rest of the season bad luck and problems of one sort or another dogged the team. After such a good first season with the team, the loss of Jacky Ickx to Ferrari was no help (Ickx was to be runner-up in the World Championship for the second year in succession) and the 44-year-old Brabham carried most of the burden himself, finishing equal fifth with Jackie Stewart in the Championship race, behind Rindt (sadly the first posthumous Champion), Ickx, Regazzoni and Hulme.

'Black Jack' had a win, two seconds and a third to his credit, earned pole position once and had four fastest laps for a total of 25 points. He was desperately unlucky in the British Grand Prix, running out of fuel on the last corner to give Rindt the victory. Strong men wept that day and thousands groaned in disappointment as Jack struggled to get the car over the line before Rindt could overtake him.

Rolf Stommelen, born at Siegen, Germany, on 11 July 1943, took over the second Brabham but he was no Ickx and rather out of his depth. Just the same he managed a third and three fifth places which gave him ten points and eleventh position in the title race. Even with that he had some illustrious names behind him, including Graham Hill, Bruce McLaren, Mario Andretti, John Surtees and Dan Gurney. But Jack must have considered ruefully that three of the first four pilots were ex-Brabham 'works' drivers – Rindt, Ickx and Hulme.

Just before taking part in the Mexican Grand Prix, Jack Brabham announced his retirement and pending return to his homeland. His name would remain familiar to the public by the continuance of the Brabham Racing Organisation; by a bend at the Brands Hatch circuit and an impressive modern structure of steel, glass and brick – the Brabham Centre – at the same circuit; and by a knighthood from Her Majesty the Queen.

The decision changed the direction of many people's lives. Not least Betty Brabham, Jack's wife, who found welcome relief from the fear which haunts the wives of so many racing-drivers – she admitted to being 'scared stiff' before every race. It was not to be a lasting relief, however, because the Brabhams had three sons . . .

For Jack himself it meant a new way of life but, if anything, he became busier than ever. He had an interest in a garage business when first he returned to Australia but he gave that up and bought a big farm, about seven hours drive from Sydney. Today, he still has that farm covering thousands of acres (although he did sell off a piece of it) and is more fortunate than many Australian farmers in that his property is on the edge of a river so that he can get water easily. In fact, he has a very splendid piece of Victoriana standing in the undergrowth – a wood-burning water-pump – but at the moment he gets his water out of the river, using a Volkswagen engine to motivate a pump.

There is an airstrip leading up to the front door, Jack being a keen pilot. He has also been interested in developing micro-light aircraft in Australia – not the motorised hang-glider type of thing but a proper light aircraft in miniature. He uses the prototype to round up cattle on the farm. It covers a big area and flying is the quickest way to get round it.

Jack's interests don't end there. He has a garage in Chessington,

'Black Jack' retired (and with a waistline to prove it) gives some advice to Colin Chapman, of Lotus, the car of Italian-American World Champion, Mario Andretti, in the foreground.

England, a Mazda franchise (and another back home) and is a partner of John Judd's in an engine development firm at Rugby, which has a fine reputation for preparing Cosworth engines. He maintains his connections with Honda and is one of their consultants. He was the spearhead for a very successful advertising campaign for Goodyear in Australia and he used to come over to Europe – to Luxembourg where Goodyear have a proving ground – and set up television advertising and the like.

Jack is always going round the world, coming to Europe a lot and visiting England two or three times a year. He's active and interested in life, in fact his only real problem is that years of racing have taken a physical toll – he wears a hearing aid and his knees are in a bad state, basically where they have been knocked about. He's seen one of the finest specialists in England but nothing much can be done about it.

The three boys spent their formative years on the farm, driving around the countryside on their motor-cycles. Geoffrey, the eldest, is now well-established in motor racing in the USA, has won quite a few events and put up an impressive performance in the Indianapolis 500. He's married and lives in California.

As this is written, 21-year-old Gary is racing in England. In 1984 he drove one of the Team Reynard cars in the British 2000 Championship and he won the 53-lap Thundersports Endurance race at Snetterton.

Yet it does not seem all that long ago that they used to go with their mother to watch their father race, two quiet and rather shy youngsters who seemed unlikely to follow in father's footsteps.

David, the baby of the family, looked at one time as if he would be the farmer of the three and he showed much more interest in the farm and its activities than did his brothers. Then someone gave him a kart and, as this is written, he is the Australian Karting Champion. Presumably, the day is not far off when he will follow father and brothers into more advanced classes of racing.

Surprise, surprise, Jack often manages to make his world tours coincide with Geoffrey or Gary racing somewhere and doubtless the boys value their Dad's advice.

Betty has three racing-drivers to worry about now instead of one and not long ago she wrote jokingly to a friend, 'I'm sitting on the farmhouse veranda with a shot-gun across my knees – all four of my men are away in different parts of the world.'

Even if he had no sons to perpetuate his name, it is doubtful if anyone who knew him would ever forget Sir John Brabham, his official nomenclature. He has always been a good friend to those who merit it. A quiet man, a gentleman, you won't find him mouthing obscenities in mixed company – or any other company for that matter.

Nor, friend or stranger, do you have to speak to him through an agent and pay a fat fee for an exchange of pleasantries. There was an occasion years ago when a BBC producer telephoned the present writer to ask if he could suggest a racing-driver who would agree to appear on a radio programme – usual BBC fees.

Thinking to do a favour for a young up-and-coming driver I put forward a certain name. Five minutes later an aggressive agent was on the line demanding large fees. Pointing out briefly and forcibly that it mattered not a jot whether his client appeared or not, the phone went down. Jack Brabham was contacted; he did the broadcast for the usual fee; and the BBC were delighted. Said the producer, 'What a co-operative man and what a decent feller. He does motor racing great credit.'

Jack and the late Graham Hill, one introvert, the other extrovert, were alike in this respect – if they could do a favour for a chum, they did not put a price tag on it. (How paths cross: in 1984, Gary, Jack's second son, would be racing against 25-year-old Damon, Graham's son, at Brands Hatch.)

One year when Jack was World Champion, his friend Dean Delamont, of the RAC, approached him. Jack Warner, 'PC Dixon of Dock Green', had agreed to present the awards at the RAC's road safety competition, 'The L-Driver of the Year'. At the last moment, the genial Mr Warner, another of nature's gentlemen, had to cry off. Jack Brabham took his place without a moment's hesitation. No, he did not want a fee. Dean was a pal. And Jack was quite embarrassed when the organisers gave him a leather wallet as a token of appreciation.

Dean says now, 'Pound notes weren't the first thing Jack looked at. He looked at them, looked at them pretty carefully in fact, but there is a difference between that and making it obvious to the world that all you are interested in is the money.'

4

A MAN CALLED TAURANAC

He's tough, speaks his mind, doesn't suffer fools gladly and wouldn't know where to begin if he was asked to tell anything but the truth. He also likes being boss of his own show which makes it somewhat of a surprise that he worked in happy harmony with Jack Brabham for so many years. It also explains why later on he started all over again – alone, save for his loyal wife.

This is Ron Tauranac, long-time partner of Jack Brabham and the man most affected when 'Black Jack' decided to quit. He had to make a big decision – to join with Jack and sell the business lock, stock and barrel, or to soldier on alone, buying Jack's share of the business.

No one knows except Mr and Mrs Tauranac how much debate went into that decision but, in the upshot, Ron decided to carry on if possible. Friends being friends, Jack and Ron had the company valued and Ron paid Jack exactly 50 per cent for his share of the business.

Solving one problem automatically brought others in its train. Ron needed a driver to replace Jack and although the German, Stommelen, had had his moments during the 1970 season, he didn't really look like a winner. Also, at 27, whilst not old for a Grand Prix driver, Rolf seemed unlikely to develop beyond the point he'd reached.

The Brabham team had been built around the anchor of Jack himself, one of the most experienced drivers in the business, backed up in the best years by New Zealander Denny Hulme who had come up through the junior ranks to Formula One.

Ron decided on the same prescription the 1971 Brabham team. He found experience in the person of Graham Hill, World Champion in 1962 and 1968. Hill, a Londoner then aged 42, just a couple of years younger than Jack, had started as a mechanic, got a job at Lotus and entered the Grand Prix scene when the Colin Chapman outfit went into Formula One in 1958. BRM signed him in 1960 and two years later he won his first world title with them. In 1967 he went back to Lotus and the following season gained his second Championship. At the end of 1969 he was so badly smashed up in a crash that there were doubts about his survival. Certainly no one expected him to race again. They underrated the man. Hours of physiotherapy and bags of determination saw him ready to race again in 1970 when he took a Lotus into the first six on four occasions. This was the man who Tauranac chose to replace Brabham.

Experience thus taken care of, Ron turned his attention to the occupant of the second car and, not surprisingly perhaps, looked to an Australian. Tim Schenken, born in Sydney on 26 September 1943, was highly thought of by many of the experts and he had been British Formula Ford Champion in 1969.

On paper it looked a balanced team and for Hill, Tauranac designed a new car, 'the lobster claw' BT34, which attracted much attention because of its unusual shape.

Unfortunately Hill, the oldest driver in Grand Prix racing now that Brabham had gone, was no longer a winner (although he was to be triumphant in the Le Mans 24-hour race the following year) and neither was the car. Graham gained one fifth place and earned but two points to finish twenty-first in the Drivers' Championship; a big comedown for a man who had twice been World Champion. He was, however, in surprisingly good company. Below him was Jean-Pierre Beltoise (Matra-Simca) with only one point, immediately above him two former world motor-cycling champions. John Surtees and Mike Hailwood, both with three points; and Surtees, of course, had also been world car Grand Prix champion.

Schenken did a little better, raising hopes with a third place, but having only one other scoring finish, a sixth place, which gave him fourteenth position in the Championship.

Jackie Stewart (Tyrrell) with 62 points, nearly twice as many as runner-up Ronnie Peterson (March) was a runaway winner.

Looked at in bald statistics it was a disastrous season, but things are rarely all black or white and there were some hopeful signs, not least that Brabham continued to sell racing cars all over the world. And if Graham Hill, not to mention 'the lobster claw', had not been amongst Ron's brightest ideas, the 'experts' were enthusiastic enough about Schenken's first year in Grand Prix racing to hail him as Jack Brabham's eventual successor.

To be accurate, it was Schenken's first full season as a 'works' driver – he had had four starts and four retirements in 1970 when he drove for the De Tomaso team, run by Frank Williams, after the talented Piers Courage had been killed in the Dutch Grand Prix.

It hadn't been a decision that Tauranac had rushed. Schenken, on his own admission, had been pestering Ron for a drive for a long time, having driven for the marque in Formula Two and Formula Three, but it wasn't until just a week before the first Formula One race of the year, the non-Championship Race of Champions at Brands Hatch, that Tauranac agreed to a 'one off'. Just before the race started Ron asked Tim if his US visa was up to date and after the Brands race he found himself flying to America, where he finished fifth in a Formula One race on the new Ontario track (not Ontario, Canada, incidentally).

Next, Tauranac asked him to race in Spain, followed by Silverstone and Monaco. Five races now and Tim had finished in each one and had a third, a fourth and a fifth. Yet still he wasn't officially a Brabham team driver – each race had been on a 'one off' basis.

Not even the euphoria of the Silverstone meeting, the one time in the year it all seemed to come right for the Brabham team, caused Ron to lose his cool and give Tim a season-long contract. 'The lobster claw' (Graham Hill) was the winner with Schenken third. Unfortunately, the International Trophy was another non-Championship race.

The French Grand Prix – a race Schenken didn't finish – finally decided Tauranac that he wanted the Australian in the team permanently. On the Paul Ricard circuit, Schenken, from being nearly last, worked his way through the field and was fourth with five laps to go when his engine blew.

History repeated itself in the German Grand Prix. Tim was third with five laps to go when his gearbox broke. He was sixth in Germany and, finally, clicked for a third place in Austria.

Tim, at least, ended the season happily, assured that he would be in the Brabham team in 1972 and very happy with his relationship with Ron Tauranac.

Schenken liked the way Ron never took anything for granted but always had to investigate the technical reasons for any change – for better or worse. He also was able to look at problems from the driver's point of view rather than a textbook designer. But, in motor racing, nothing is ever certain . . .

Tauranac was, naturally, rather disappointed at the season's outcome from all points of view, not least the comparative failure of the BT34 the design of which he had been assisted in by another well-known draughtsman, Ray Jessop, and a young man of whom more would be heard, Gordon Murray.

A man named Bernie Ecclestone was interested in getting into Grand Prix racing. He had driven Coopers in 500 cc racing, dabbled briefly in Formula One as a potential entrant and had been Jochen Rindt's manager.

In some ways Ecclestone was just what Tauranac needed. Ron, described by John Cooper as 'a good engineer and a hard slogger', just wanted to build first-class racing cars. Lunching potential sponsors, attending board-meetings, wining and dining the Press – none of this was Ron Tauranac's style. It interfered with the job in hand. So an astute business man like Ecclestone, to whom negotiating was the meat-and-drink of life, seemed to be the answer.

There was one snag. Ecclestone and Tauranac were alike in one respect, they both liked to keep in touch with everything, but *everything*, that happened around the place and they were both by nature solo commanders. Tauranac, of whom it was once said, 'If the coffee-machine in the workshop breaks down, he'll be the first to know – and he'll probably have the best ideas on how to mend it', realised that he and Bernie could never work in double harness. Whatever the firm needed, two bosses weren't the answer. So Ron sold out ... Again the company was valued and Bernie made Ron an acceptable offer.

It was not the end of the Tauranac story. In some ways it was only the end of the beginning. It was inconceivable that the world of racing would ignore a man who had proved himself such a brilliant designer. Several teams sought Ron's advice including the up-and-coming Williams marque.

Lotus went further and Colin Chapman made overtures to add Tauranac to the Hethersett staff – a compliment indeed from a man who was a brilliant designer himself – but the offer was refused.

When Ron finally accepted a job it was because he was virtually offered a free hand, 'the own boss' syndrome again. Trojan, originally manufacturers of chain-driven solid-tyre delivery vans and subsequently of everything from chain-saws to motor scooters, asked him to design and build both a Formula One and a Formula 5000 car for 1974. Alas, the time was inopportune! There were so many makes trying to gain a slot on the Grand Prix grids that the lesser lights were being crowded out.

As for Formula 5000, of which much had been expected, it virtually fizzled out, largely due to the fact that it was nearly as expensive as Grand Prix racing and not nearly as rewarding.

This was a pity. Given a year or two, Ron might well have produced another World Championship winner. But it was not to be ...

However, there were ex-Brabham customers around who wanted new cars - and the magic touch of Tauranac to go with them. Approached to build a Formula Three car, Ron's thoughts went back to Australia ... He built his first racing car back in the 1940s, a single-seater with a 500 cc motor-cycle engine, not dissimilar from the cars which were to re-establish motor racing in Britain after the Second World War. Ron's younger brother, Austen Lewis Tauranac, assisted him in building the car and so when they looked for a name, they decided upon their own initials R for Ron, AL for Austin Lewis and T for Tauranac. Thus the Ralt Mk. 1 came into being.

Other Ralts followed including a sports-car with a Ford Ten engine and a variety of single-seaters, until the day when Jack Brabham persuaded his old rival to come to England and join forces in Motor Racing Developments.

So the Ralt was born again. First of the new breed, the Ralt RT1 went to another Australian driver, Larry Perkins, who promptly proceeded to win the European Cup with it. Orders came in thick and fast, the versatile Ralt being suited not only for Formula Three, for which it had been designed, but also Formula Two and Formula Atlantic. The influx of business was such that Ron took the old Brabham workshops at New Haw, near Weybridge, to build Ralts and is still there to this day.

Altogether, 150 Ralt RTs were built and at the same time Tauranac worked on a Formula One project for the Teddy Yip team. In 1979, emulating the Grand Prix boys, he introduced 'ground effect' Ralts for Formula Two, Formula Three, Formula Atlantic and Formula Super Vee - sometime Grand Prix driver Brian Henton doing very well in the European Formula Two Championship with an RT2.

Today, Ralts are probably the most successful racing cars in the world.

Britain's brightest young hope, Johnny Dumfries, has dominated the British and European Formula Three Championships in a Volkswagen-Ralt. Off the track, Johnny is the Earl of Dumfries, heir to the Marquis of Bute. Married and the father of a baby daughter, he makes no secret of his ambition to be a Grand Prix driver.

Graham Hill at Zandvoort in 1971. The car is the ill-fated Brabham BT 34, the 'lobster claw' as it was called owing to its unusual design.

Ron Tauranac, after his achievements in designing Brabham cars, proved it was no fluke by starting all over again with a winning range of Ralt cars. Here, Johnny Dumfries wins at Donington Park, March 1984, in a Team BP Volkswagen Ralt.

Ralts have also been behind the success of Murray Taylor, a New Zealander who went via the RAC Press Office and the newspaper, *Motoring News*, surviving a horrendous car crash along the way, to run, with the aid of wife Glenys, one of the top teams outside Grand Prix racing.

The 1984 European Formula Two Championship fell to the Ralt-Honda V6 team (patron and director Ron Tauranac) with New Zealander Mike Thackwell as champion and his team-mate, Brazilian Roberto Moreno, as runner-up. In what was to be the last year of the Formula (it being replaced by Formula 3000 in 1985), the Ralt-Hondas won no less than nine of the eleven races, with Thackwell, who has made spasmodic appearances on the Grand Prix circuit, winning seven of them. Furthermore, Moreno, the man whom Nelson Piquet thinks should be in Grand Prix racing, backed him up well.

In practice on the Brands Hatch Grand Prix circuit, Thackwell has lapped his Ralt-Honda in 1 minute, 17.5 seconds, a time which would have put him comfortably on the grid for the British Grand Prix itself.

The battle between Ron Tauranac's two drivers was usually the most exciting feature of the Formula Two season, since their cars were superior to anything else in the field. As *Autocar* put it, 'Ron Tauranac, the man who does Formula Two best.'

Certainly, Tauranac has proved himself a man for all seasons and for all types of racing. It may well be that posterity will make him one of the truly great racing-car designers of all time ...

Some of the associations formed by Ron Tauranac remain with the Brabham team to this day. Koni, the Dutch shock-absorber firm, represented in the UK by Banks of Peterborough, during 1984 celebrated the 200th win by Grand Prix cars fitted with their equipment and one of the teams that has contributed most to that proud record is Brabham.

Aert van der Goes, Koni's Racing Services Manager, says: 'Our first meeting with Mr R.S. Tauranac was at the London Motor Show in 1964. It was three years later - on 6 February 1967- that a Brabham Formula Two car, fitted with our dampers, was tested at Goodwood by Jack Brabham himself. The tests were successful and an order followed.'

Later that year, in May, as a result of Mario Andretti's experiences of Indianapolis, Ron Tauranac ordered several more dampers and early in 1968, more were ordered for use at Indy. At the German and Italian Grands Prix that year, the Brabhams ran on Koni.

The following year (1969) Tauranac was obviously 'sold' on the idea that Koni were best for the Brabham cars. He ordered 22 for Formula One and Indy. Jacky Ickx won the German Grand Prix and was second in the British, using the equipment.

Ralph Bellamy, who designed the Brabham BT37, said he preferred Koni to Armstrong, which were used spasmodically, because he found them easier to adjust.

From 1970 onwards, Koni has been used on all Brabham Formula One and Formula Two cars.

5

MURRAY AND THE SOUTH AMERICAN WAY

The man who spans the Brabham, Tauranac and Ecclestone eras at Motor Racing Developments is South African-born Gordon Murray. He joined Brabham in 1970, working on production cars (which Bernie Ecclestone was to cease manufacturing in 1973), modifying the first monocoque, the BT33, assisting Ron Tauranac and Ray Jessop with the BT34 and Ralph Bellamy with the BT37.

During the next decade Murray was to emerge as a truly outstanding Grand Prix designer. It was his triangular monocoque, the BT42, which was to bring the Brabham team out of the wilderness and the BT44, which replaced it for 1974, was a winner in the hands of the Argentinian driver, Carlos Reutemann.

Murray's philosophy: 'Most things in engineering which *are* right, *look* right. Beauty in car design to me is simplicity and cleanliness. Bad design means a clash of lines and planes, embellishment for it's own sake, lack of "feel" for an overall balance, often a "committee" design'. But he added, 'I find cars beautiful for different reasons – they need to be judged beautiful for the type of car they are.'

It was a philosophy which would be given plenty of opportunity for expression in the ensuing years, but before that could happen the 1972 season loomed ominously close.

The team faced that prospect with a new owner, a man who had raced – but only in the immediate post-war half-litre class; a man who had owned Grand Prix cars before – but only Connaughts after that team expired for want of cash; a revolutionary car – which had been pretty much of a flop in its first season; and uncertainties as to who would occupy the driving-seats.

Ecclestone, like Tauranac before him, decided to go along with the experience of Graham Hill, a great driver past his best, but Schenken was replaced by Reutemann, who had been sponsored by fellow-Argentinians in attempting a break-through in European racing.

Riccardo Patrese, the dare-devil driver who partnered Piquet in the Brabham team during the 1983 season and was succeeded by the Fabi brothers in 1984.

In pensive mood: the Brabham pit at Brands Hatch, 1984. Brabham designer Gordon Murray (with the clipboard) consults with members of the pit crew whilst assembled photographers look appropriately solemn.

The departure of Schenken was something else. In the end it was his own decision. The Australian was unhappy at the turn of events and decided to take an offer to go to Surtees. Hill, on the other hand, was pleased to have a second year with Brabham. It was an open secret around the circuit that although Tauranac and Hill had started their partnership with high hopes it had gone a little sour by season's end for no other reason than that both were strongminded men with their own opinions on the best way of dealing with things.

Schenken's replacement, Carlos Reutemann, born in Sante Fé on 12 April 1942, had done well with a Formula Two Brabham in 1971 and was eventually to come within a whisker of the world title, a Grand Prix driver of distinction who, perhaps, failed at the final hurdle because of temperament.

The ill-fated 'lobster claw' was discarded. Hill began the season with a modified BT33 and Reutemann had the 1972 design, the BT37, to which Hill later switched. During the year, a prototype BT39 was produced, powered by a Weslake–Ford 190, 2995 cc and twelve cylinders. The car was never raced.

Confronted by Lotus, Tyrrell, McLaren and Ferrari, all at the pinnacle of achievement, the Brabhams stood not a chance and were most of the time scrapping with an assortment of Surtees, Matras, Marches and BRMs for the minor placings. Emerson Fittipaldi (Lotus 72) won five races, finished second in two and was third in another to skate the Championship with 61 points to the 45 of Jackie Stewart (Tyrrell). Jackie, who won four races, was reckoned the highest-paid driver in the sport at £250,000 a year.

The only other winners, with one victory apiece, were Hulme (McLaren), Ickx (Ferrari) and Beltoise (BRM).

Hill tied for twelfth place in the Championship with Mario Andretti, the Italian–American Indianapolis winner (Ferrari), New Zealander Howden Ganley (BRM) and Brian Redman (McLaren). The veteran Londoner had one fifth place and two sixth places for four points.

Reutemann, giving a hint of things to come by gaining the pole position in one race, had a fourth place and three points, sharing sixteenth position with Italy's Andrea de Adamich (Surtees) and the Brazilian Carlos Pace (March).

1973 saw Murray's 'triangular' creation take the field, the first of some remarkable cars with which the tall, thin, moustachioed designer would stagger, shake and sometimes annoy the Grand Prix circus in the next decade.

Hill had gone to the Embassy Shadow team so Reutemann became No. 1 driver and in the BT42 he looked a man to be reckoned with, finishing seventh in the Championship behind Stewart, Emerson Fittipaldi, Ronnie Peterson, François Cevert (unfortunately killed at the tail-end of the season), Peter Revson and Denny Hulme. The good-looking South American picked up two third, two fourth and two sixth places for 16 points, a healthy score for a Brabham driver at that stage of the Grand Prix story.

Wilson Fittipaldi, given his chance by Hill's departure, is the elder brother of Emerson. A former Brazilian kart champion, he graduated to Formula One through Formula Three and Formula Two but never reached the heights during his brief sojourn in top circles, retiring from driving to develop his own team, Copersucar Fittipaldi, which, despite having Emerson as No. 1 driver, never became a major threat.

The elder Fittipaldi started the 1973 season in a BT37 before he too was given a BT42. He picked up a fifth and sixth place, was fifteenth in the table and can truthfully claim that in his only full Grand Prix season he finished ahead of Niki Lauda (BRM), Clay Regazzoni (BRM), Chris Amon (Tecno), van Lennep (Williams) and Howden Ganley (Williams). But for Lauda and Regazzoni, at least, the great days were yet to come, as indeed they were for the Williams team. Thus are the 'chumps' of today, the 'champs' of tomorrow – and vice versa, of course.

Gordon Murray's BT44, with the now-proven and reliable Ford DFV engine, brought a winning look back to Brabham in 1974, aided by the driving skills of Reutemann. One of the enigmas of the sport, 'Lolé', as he is known after 'El Lolé' (the bull in Spanish), first came to Britain as a sponsored young 'hope'. He spoke little English and would stand quietly by, a faint smile on his face, while more voluble members of the team practised their fractured English on his behalf. His driving improved a lot, his English more than a bit – but the enigma remained. He was to come so near to the World Championship and yet the public were left with the impression that when it counted he didn't want the title as fiercely as did some of his competitors. He just wasn't 'a hungry fighter' was the general verdict.

But all that was ahead. For the moment, the Brabham team, after seasons in the doldrums, were seeking not a Championship but just a single, solitary Grand Prix victory . . . just one.

Reutemann, now aged 32 – the prime of a Grand Prix driver's life – gave them not one but *three* such victories. In South Africa he drove brilliantly and the Brabham was uncatchable. He gave a repeat performance in the Austrian Grand Prix and led from pole to flag in the last Championship round of the season at Watkins Glen. He was also singularly unlucky in the season's opener in his native Argentina, retiring almost at the end of the race after leading most of the way.

Reutemann did pick up a third and a sixth for good measure but, not for the first time, it was to be the minor placings which would decide the title. No one else scored more than three wins – Emerson Fittipaldi and Ronnie Peterson, however, equalling 'Lolé' in this respect. Scheckter and Lauda had two victories apiece; and Clay Regazzoni and Denny Hulme one each. But it was Fittipaldi, with two second, two thirds, two fourth places and a fifth place, who took the honours; whilst the unfortunate Reutemann was only sixth in the table, an indication, not for the first time, that the scoring system might leave something to be desired.

However, for Ecclestone, Murray and the Brabham 'backroom boys' three Grand Prix wins came like finding, not an oasis in the desert, but a brewery. They really felt they were on the way back.

In addition, the Brazilian, Carlos Pace, starting the season with a Surtees TS16/2, switched to Brabham and a BT44 and collected a second, fourth and fifth place; whilst privately-entered John Watson, originally from Ulster but based in Bognor, starting with a BT42 and then a BT44, gained a fourth and fifth place.

Reutemann and Pace were to be a formidable combination in 1975, both driving updated BT44Bs. Reutemann was third in the Championship behind Lauda and Emerson Fittipaldi. Between them the South Americans had two wins, three second, four third, three fourth places and a fifth place. Pace won pole position once and set fastest lap once. All in all, thirteen scoring places in a total of fourteen races was by no means an unsatisfactory season.

In many ways, Pace, the 'other Carlos', probably gained more satisfaction from the year's racing than his team-mate because he achieved his first Grand Prix victory, fittingly in front of his hometown crowd at Interlagos. He drove fast and well in other races too but without the good fortune that every successful sportsman must have from time to

A group of motor-racing greats: Denny Hulme, 1967 World Champion with Brabham; another World Champion, Phil Hill; the legendary Stirling Moss; top pre-war driver Louis Chiron; World Champion Graham Hill, who also had a spell with Brabham; and British Grand Prix winner, Baron de Graffenreid.

Author Phil Drackett with Stirling Moss, 'One of the greatest drivers never to win the world title'. One year Moss missed the Championship by a solitary point – and won more races than anyone.

Members of the Royal Family have long been keen motor-sport enthusiasts, notably the Duke of Kent and his brother, Prince Michael, a regular rally competitor. Here, Prince Charles and Lord Mountbatten talk to Graham Hill before the 1968 British Grand Prix at Brands Hatch.

time. Reutemann, on the other hand, although winning the German Grand Prix at the Nürburgring, had one or two of those 'lapses' which were to haunt him all through his career.

When the season opened in Argentina, the world saw the consequences of the winter work put in by Brabham owner Bernie Ecclestone and designer Gordon Murray. Ecclestone had secured major sponsorship from Martini and support from the FINA fuel company and the Brabham team had three smart new livery cars available for practice. Reutemann's was a brand-new BT44B with stiffer chassis, altered suspension, a revised nose-piece and narrower front track. The other two were BT44s, but substantially rebuilt.

That was the good news. The bad news soon followed. The car that Lolé drove broke down in practice. Pace practised in both models and wasn't happy with either. The B, he opined, was quicker in a straight line than the ordinary 44 but lazy about turning corners at high speed. The chunky-built Brazilian was feeling a bit sour about life in general. The previous season he had complained that his seat was too tight and hurt his ribs and although a new seat had been moulded for him the practice sessions again left him bruised around the ribs. He went to hospital for a pain-killing injection.

Lolé made a good start in the race and led for much of the way, hotly pursued by his team-mate but however much 'Carlos the First' wanted to win his native Grand Prix the car faltered and it was not to be. Nor was 'Carlos the Second', otherwise known as 'Moco', to win, his engine stopping when he was in fourth place and going well. In the end, Fittipaldi (McLaren) won with James Hunt (Hesketh) second and Reutemann third.

Tyres were the dominating factor in Brazil. With *all* the cars on Goodyear tyres, the choice was between the softer 'Argentine' tyre and a harder compound especially designed for the Brazilian circuit. Despite this some of the drivers went faster on the 'Argentine' version.

When the flag dropped, Pace took a tight grip on his fiery nature and was there to take advantage when Jean-Pierre Jarier's leading UOP stopped on the circuit with only eight laps to go. Moco held off the challenge of fellow-Brazilian Emerson Fittipaldi to win by five seconds, his first World Championship victory. The Brabham team were more than pleased – a successful and 'busy' Grand Prix had been negotiated despite two of the mechanics being down with illness, increasing the work-load of the rest.

Poor old Pace was almost torn from his car by enthusiastic compatriots, his overalls were ripped and he was hoisted high in the air. Just for good measure, an excited radio commentator managed to hit him in the mouth with a 'mike'.

Reutemann, who had won the race in 1972 when it was a non-Championship affair, could do no better than eighth this time.

There was a month's gap before the South African Grand Prix where Brabham again appeared with three BT44Bs, the only alteration from Brazil being some additional little aerodynamic 'air-dams'.

Tyres were again much under discussion, there being four kinds of Goodyear available. Pace had one or two troubles in practice – once the mechanics had to hump a fuel churn and battery out to him in very hot weather – but when the grid was published there was Pace on the pole with Reutemann alongside. Gordon Murray, naturally hopeful for a win in his own country, was very happy at this stage: 'All the changes we made to the car this year were to improve its slow-speed corner-characteristics and I guess we're quite happy that we seem not to have harmed the high-speed behaviour.'

South Africa's Jody Scheckter (Tyrrell-Ford) looked a runaway winner early on, but midway Reutemann was gaining on him steadily. The gap came down to a second but then the Argentinian had trouble getting past some of the back-markers and the gap widened a little. Behind, a similar Tyrrell versus Brabham battle was going on for third place between Depailler and Pace, but again it was the Tyrrell which managed to hold on, the Brabhams having to be content with second and fourth.

The less said about the Spanish Grand Prix which followed the better. Officially Mass (McLaren) was first, Ickx (John Player Special) second and Reutemann third but only half-points were awarded.

The whole affair was a shambles. Drivers were unhappy about the safety barriers and most of them boycotted practice, Ickx and Brambilla being the exceptions. Then the organisers threatened to have the cars impounded by the police so the drivers reluctantly went out for the last practice session. Emerson Fittipaldi, the reigning champion, refused to start the race. His brother, Wilson, started but retired after one lap. So did Arturo Merzario. They were well out of it. Ten cars were involved in accidents and when finally one went off into the crowd, killing four people, the race *was* stopped.

A grisly chain of cause and effect is seen in the reasons for some of the retirements: Stommelen (Hill) – accident, lost rear wing; Pace (Brabham) – accident, avoiding Stommelen; Peterson (JPS) – accident, collided with Migault; Pryce (Shadow) – in pits, following collision with Brise; Andretti (Parnelli) – accident, collision on first lap; Hunt (Hesketh) – accident, spun on oil; Donohue (Penske) – accident, spun on oil from Scheckter's engine; Jones (Hesketh) – accident, hit by Donohue; Depailler (Tyrrell) – accident, collision on first lap; and Lauda (Ferrari) – accident, hit by Andretti on first lap.

It must all have been very different when Carlos de Salamanca, driving a Rolls-Royce, won the first Spanish Grand Prix in 1913 at a speed of 54 mph!

The next race was at Monaco and the organisers were taking no chances. The field was cut to eighteen starters and the grid spaced out so as to reduce the likelihood of an early shunt. Even so, nine of the eighteen failed to finish, six of them being involved in accidents.

Pace again went well, finishing third, 18 seconds behind the winner, Lauda, and 15 seconds behind second-placed Fittipaldi. Reutemann, ninth and last of the official finishers, was two laps behind.

Lauda made it two in a row in Belgium – something no driver had accomplished for two years – but Reutemann was third and Pace, a lap behind, eighth. At this stage of the season, Brabham consistency was paying off and the team led McLaren for the Constructors' Championship with Reutemann and Pace equal third in the Drivers'.

Lauda completed his hat-trick in Sweden after Reutemann had led for most of the way. Worsening over-steer and increasing wear on the rear tyres forced the Brabham driver to be content with second place. Pace went out on Lap 41 when he spun and hit the fence.

Reutemann was now second in the title race with Pace fourth. Brabham were well clear of McLaren in the Constructors' Cup but Lauda's persistent success meant that Ferrari moved up to share the lead.

Gordon was still trying ideas to get a bit more out of the Brabhams. The cars were back on Girling brakes for the Dutch Grand Prix and the designer tried a new airbox orifice, labelled for want of a better word, 'the splitter', and described by someone as 'a sort of nose with a nostril either side'. Which makes one wonder what sort of people *he* knows!

The problems of a designer were never better illustrated. Reutemann tried the device and pronounced a distinct improvement in maximum revs; Pace tried it and reported a distinct deterioration in maximum revs. Carlos used it in the race, the 'other Carlos' didn't.

Both went well; Reutemann finishing fourth and Pace fifth. Ferraris had walked it the previous year and the 1975 race was again tipped to be a Ferrari benefit. Lauda and Regazzoni did finish in front of the Brabhams but Lauda lost first place by not much more than a second to James Hunt and Hesketh, whose first Grand Prix victory it was.

It meant that Ferrari eased ahead of Brabham in the manufacturers' battle while the two Carloses stayed second and fourth in their particular struggle.

Round nine was the French Grand Prix and with Brabhams so well situated, Gordon Murray made only detail amendments to the two race cars although the practice car appeared with cycle-type front wings for the stated purpose of preventing stones being thrown up at the driver.

The race wasn't one to remember for Bernie's boys. Lauda won again which put him far out in front and gave Ferrari a commanding lead too.

The British Grand Prix at Silverstone provided one sensation after another. *Sixteen* drivers crashed and when the race was finally abandoned with most of the survivors on what appeared to be Lap 55 – or was it Lap 56? – arguments raged for hours as to who had finished in which position.

Lolé could survey it with a detached air. For once his engine let him down and he retired on Lap 4 so he missed the fun and games which caused the race to be red-flagged after most of the survivors slid off or crashed in the rain.

Pace was right in there, however, and was eventually placed second to Fittipaldi, the only driver in the race who appeared to avoid all mishaps whether acts of manufacturers, mechanics or God.

Reutemann was now joint third with Hunt in the Drivers' Championship, Pace fifth, and Brabham had closed the gap on Ferrari in the Constructors' Cup.

The Nürburgring was another disastrous race, though of a different kind to the Spanish and the British Grands Prix. Stones and debris on the circuit caused an epidemic of punctures – at least twelve – causing two crashes and six retirements. Only nine of the 24 starters were running at the finish and of these only two had had a trouble-free race – the winner Lolé (his first Grand Prix victory of the year) and Jacques Laffite (Williams) who was more than $1\frac{1}{2}$ minutes behind the Martini–Brabham.

Reutemann's win was in the car with which he had started the season but Pace had a new car, the fourth BT44B, which had been completed earlier in the season. He went out on Lap 5 with a broken rear upright.

The win put Lolé back in second pace, although trailing Lauda by 17 points, with Pace fifth – and Brabham were right on Ferrari's heels.

Another half-race followed. It rained so heavily and became so dangerous at the Austrian Grand Prix that the race was halted after 29 laps, half-points being awarded. The 37-year-old Vittorio Brambilla (March-Ford) charged from the eighth row of the grid to lead by Lap 19. Ten laps later he had increased his lead to 24 seconds and was so surprised to find the chequered flag waved at him that he lost control and spun into the guard-rail, acknowledging the cheers of the crowd from a car definitely shorn of its pristine glory!

Pace had gone out with engine trouble on Lap 17 and Reutemann was a lap behind Brambilla, in fourteenth place, when the race was halted. Lauda picked up one half-point for sixth place so the result made little difference to either Championship.

Murray had taken along a new design of rear aerofoil but it was not used – time not permitting such luxuries as experiments. One of the three Brabhams broke a crown-wheel in practice and a second, driven by Pace, lost a wheel when the left rear stub-axle sheared. The car spun and came to a halt but the wheel bounded into the crowd at something like 100 mph. Fortunately only one spectator was injured and then only slightly.

Race day started as badly as it possibly could when, during unofficial practice, the American Mark Donohue crashed into the fencing. He was severely injured as were two marshals. Donohue and one of the marshals later died.

The Brabham team still had some minor dramas to come before the race began. Reutemann's car sprang a fuel-bag leak while Pace's had a crank-case oil leak. In the race itself, both drivers reported their cars 'veering' and it was found that in all the pre-race hullabaloo the tyres of the two cars had been mixed up.

Although there were two rounds to go, the next one, the Italian Grand Prix at Monza, settled all major issues. Regazzoni won for Ferrari with Lauda third. It meant world titles for both the Austrian driver and the Italian team. Reutemann *had to win* to preserve his chances but just didn't have the speed; he was also hampered with braking problems.

Leading the pack: a familiar scene as a Parmalat–Brabham screams through the Silverstone chicane well ahead of all pursuers.

Carlos Pace, driving a Martini–Brabham BT44B, shows a clean pair of rear tyres to a rival, during the Spanish Grand Prix of 1975.

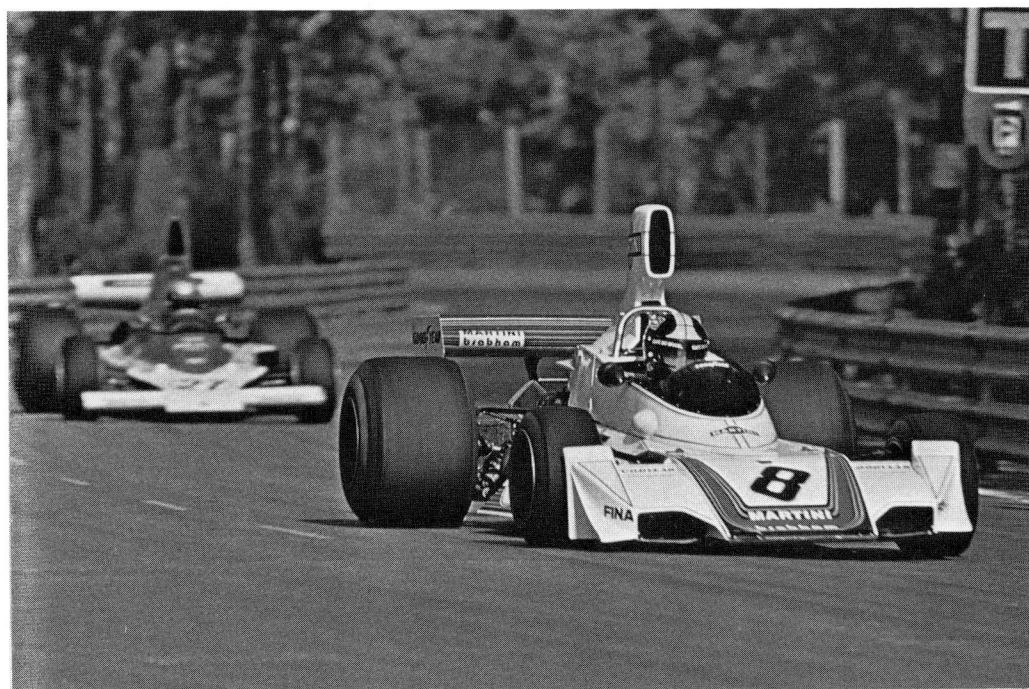

Pace's bad luck continued and he went out with a broken throttle connection.

The final round at Watkins Glen didn't matter too much. But it did bring more controversy to a season which had already seen enough. Lauda won again but Regazzoni, his team-mate, was black-flagged for persistently baulking Fittipaldi, the only man who seemed likely to catch the Austrian, whilst the Ferrari team manager and the Clerk of the Course engaged in a bit of sparring.

The Brabhams had their underside air-dams fitted but not for long. They were removed after the first practice. In the race itself it was almost as if the cars, like the mechanical marvel in the popular TV series 'Knight Rider', could think and had realised the race was but an academic exercise – Pace's machine collided with Depailler's Tyrrell on the second lap and both went out whilst engine trouble forced Lolé's retirement seven laps later.

All in all, 1975 had been a very good season for the team that Bernie built and Gordon Murray designed; and the following year looked full of promise. But it had been a black season for motor racing in general and it ended that way when former Brabham driver Graham Hill and members of his Embassy team, including the promising British driver Tony Brise, were killed when the plane the ex-World Champion was piloting crashed in fog a short distance from his Hertfordshire home.

The off-season was a busy one for Gordon Murray and the workshop force. The BT45 was produced, designed to take a new Alfa-Romeo 115 12-cylinder engine of 2993 cc – apart from anything else a step quite understandable in view of the team's Italian sponsorship – but this was to prove little short of disastrous to what looked on paper a winning team: a shrewd owner, Bernie Ecclestone; a clever designer, Gordon Murray; one of the finest pit crews in the business; and two South America drivers, one already established as a top-liner, the other showing even more promise.

As often happens, the new power-plant had its teething troubles: unfortunately, too many of them. The engine arrived with an impeccable pedigree. It had been designed by Carlo Chiti who, in five years as Ferrari's chief racing engineer, had won the Italian team two World Championships. When he moved to Alfa-Romeo his flat-12 engine won Alfa the World Sports Car Championship in 1975 (and a turbo-charged version was to do so again in 1977). Chiti developed a Formula One version of this engine and it was this power-plant that Brabham were to rely on in 1976.

It was not to be a very satisfactory year and yet, in a stormy and dramatic season there was plenty to distract public attention from the short-comings, accidental, inevitable and sometimes more than unpredictable, of the Brabham team.

The Argentine race was cancelled and so the Brazilian Grand Prix became the first of the season. Pace, winner the previous year, had the original BT45 whilst Reutemann had BT45/2.

In order to try and improve fuel consumption, Murray had fitted SPICA fuel injection units to the Alfa engines but these were rather bulky and Lucas units were fitted for the race. The new cars appeared to be overweight and although the sweating Brabham mechanics worked with might and main nothing they could do seemed to produce the desired results. It seemed extremely unlikely that the Alfa-powered cars could do anything to upset the established machines like those of Ferrari, Tyrrell, etc., and so it proved.

Lauda (Ferrari), Depailler (Tyrrell-Ford) and Pryce (Shadow-Ford) were the first three home, Pace being a lap behind in tenth place. The Brazilian driver couldn't get maximum revs for his car, which was perhaps just as well since Reutemann ran out of fuel on Lap 37.

Six weeks later the teams met in South Africa, Brabham's having been very busy in the interim. The cars were lighter – more titanium in the chassis, more magnesium castings in the engine – but everything else was much the same, alterations to the suspension and the double airbox layout having had no effect, the cars had been returned to original design in those respects.

Reutemann was pretty quick in practice but some sort of hoodoo seemed to be on the team: Pace's car, which had been going well, suddenly stuttered and Moco had to borrow Lolé's machine.

When race time came round, Lolé, that Jekyll-and-Hyde of Grand Prix drivers, was driving *off* the circuit in a desperate bid to take the lead, but before long both Brabhams were spewing oil, much to the discomfort of drivers in their vicinity. It could not last and first Lolé and then Moco retired, but at least there had been signs of improved performance from the cars.

The very first United States Grand Prix West, held at Long Beach, California, was next on the calendar. Regazzoni, racing for Ferrari, won

A one-time Grand Prix monopoly by Goodyear tyres resulted in this unusual shot of 22 top drivers in Brazil. They are from left to right - *standing*: Wilds, Depailler, Pryce, W. Fittipaldi*, Ickx*, Chrobak (Goodyear International Racing Manager), Stommelen*, Scheckter, Hill*, Lauda*, Pace*, E. Fittipaldi*, Hunt, Mass; *sitting*: Peterson, Jarier,

Laffite, Merzario, Donohue, Regazzoni, Reutemann*, Andretti, Watson*. Those marked with an asterisk were either Brabham drivers of the past or present or were later to become Brabham drivers.

unchallenged from the pole with his team-mate Lauda content with second place.

Gordon Murray, whom one would have thought had enough problems on his plate, spoke with the zeal of a true enthusiast when asked to comment on this new street circuit: 'I'd like to see a few more circuits like this. We've become just a little complacent, I believe. We've had such a generally good reliability record over the past couple of years and we've got the cars to perform so well on our regular circuits that I think we'd be better for a little stirring up with this sort of challenge.'

The team arrived in Long Beach with three BT45s, the newest one having a chassis 10 kilogrammes lighter and with even more weight saved in the engine compartment. All three cars were on Lucas injection. The ill-luck, if it can be called that, continued. Moco had an engine blow up in practice, Lolé hit a barrier. When the race started, Lolé didn't even complete the first lap, a 'coming together' with Brambilla putting them both out. Pace hung in there but was three laps behind at the finish, being placed ninth.

Spain was next and again the scene of controversy. James Hunt won; was disqualified because his McLaren was ruled to be one half-inch too wide; saw Lauda installed as winner: and two months later was reinstated. Unnoticed in the uproar concerning the effect of the new regulations, the Brabhams, whilst not pulling up any trees, had their best 1976 results yet. Reutemann, despite complaining of *oversteer*, finished fourth; Pace, despite complaining of *understeer*, finished sixth.

Murray approached the Belgian Grand Prix with more confidence. 'They've got the engines going pretty well ['they' being the Alfa-Romeo mechanics] so we are concentrating on the chassis. We've improved the front suspension and hope to do likewise with the rear.' Famous last words . . .

Belgium was a Ferrari benefit again with Lauda first, Regazzoni second and only Laffite (Ligier-Matra) and Scheckter (Tyrrell-Ford) on the same lap. Reutemann retired with engine trouble on Lap 17, Pace, after charging well, went out on Lap 58 with bother in the electrics.

So to Monaco, a race which still retains a certain magic. But not, on this occasion, for the Brabham team. Stiffened rear suspension and six-speed gearboxes (Reutemann decided against using one in the race) were not enough. For the second time in the season, Lolé did not even complete a lap, he and Alan Jones colliding at the first chicane. Pace did rather better, completing 76 laps, two less than the winner, to be placed ninth.

It almost goes without saying that the winner was Lauda, the Ferrari being followed home by the six-wheeled Tyrrells of Scheckter and Depailler.

The remarkable six-wheelers scored a 1–2 in the Swedish Grand Prix, Lauda being relegated to third place. For Brabham it was an all too familiar story. Reutemann, driving the spare car, after his own was badly damaged in practice when Scheckter put him into the wall, retired on Lap 2 with valve trouble. Pace was eighth and last of the cars to be on the same lap as the leader when the flag fell.

Between each race, the work of trying to improve the cars went on. For the French Grand Prix, the rising-rate linkage of the front suspension had been altered as had the settings of the rear suspension. The constant tinkering with the airboxes had produced yet another version with larger inlet areas to improve acceleration. There were fans to cool the brakes, deep skirting all round the chassis and streamlining discs on the front wheels. In the first timed practice, Moco was fastest with 177.36 mph, but Lolé's engine ceased functioning on one cylinder after only three laps. Pace's engine then faltered and both cars were fitted with new ones. Neither driver was particularly happy and eventually Reutemann's car had yet another engine installed. On top of everything else, the big Argentinian was still nursing a hand injured in his Swedish crash.

In the sequel, scrutineering and the new regulations overshadowed the race itself. Watson (Penske) was disqualified after a Brabham protest about his car (and was to be reinstated following Hunt's reinstatement as winner of the Spanish Grand Prix).

Lauda, for once, retired with engine trouble and Hunt took first place with Pace fourth. Reutemann, a lap behind, was eleventh.

The record books show that Lauda won the British Grand Prix at Brands Hatch. Sixty thousand or more British fans think it was James Hunt. It is a long story which properly belongs in another place. Suffice it to say that a collision between the two Ferraris soon after the start, during which Hunt was forced off the track, caused the race to be halted. When it was announced that Hunt was among those who would *not* be allowed to re-start, the boos and roars of disapproval were frightening. Had not the decision been hurriedly reversed it is likely that a section of the crowd would have taken the law into their own hands and wrecked the place. Hunt went on to 'win' but following a Ferrari protest, Lauda was awarded the race two months later.

Most disqualifications in Grand Prix racing are difficult enough for the layman to understand and usually revolve around complicated and abstruse technical regulations, which not even the designers and constructors fully understand. It is the Achilles heel of Grand Prix racing because the paying spectator wants to see races decided out on the track and not in the Committee Room and the tendency is to be sympathetic towards someone disqualified because their car was one half-inch too wide or one eighth-inch too high.

To many people. Hunt's initial exclusion and eventual disqualification was a disgrace. It was a Ferrari driver, Regazzoni, who caused all the trouble in the first place and the other driver involved was his Ferrari team-mate, Lauda. Yet it was the Ferrari team which, in the end, benefited.

The arguments were of little import to the Brabham *equipe*. Reutemann's race ended on Lap 46 – he had been losing oil from a split in the tank – and Pace finished eighth which seemed to be about par for the course for him these days.

And so to Germany, The 'Ring, and the most traumatic race of a traumatic season. Yet again there were in effect *two* races. Jochen Mass (Marlboro–McLaren) gambled on 'dry' tyres and was 29 seconds ahead after only two laps. But the race was stopped when Lauda's Ferrari went off the track and burst into flames. The Championship leader, terribly burned, was taken to hospital and the race re-started, minus six of the company.

Brabham were present with their usual three cars, Moco's machine being fitted with an air-starter system. The spare car was fitted with an experimental Dunlop braking system in which the rubbing faces of the discs were machined to take carbon fibre pucks. The team was obviously concerned about the braking troubles they had been experiencing.

Pace tried the car briefly in practice and it actually raced, the German driver Rolf Stommelen, an ex-Brabham 'works' driver who was involved in contractual difficulties elsewhere, taking the wheel.

It was another 'non-event' for Reutemann whose car 'just stopped' (engine trouble was the official reason), but Pace, despite the fact that he had been suffering from flu, drove very well and was only pipped for third place in the closing stages by Mass. Hunt was the winner with Scheckter second. Stommelen was a good sixth in the spare Brabham.

Round eleven was in Austria - without Lauda and without the Ferrari team.

Following Stommelen's creditable drive with the Dunlop experimental car, Pace drove it this time and, ironically, his race ended when the brake fluid boiled and the Brabham smashed into the barriers.

It was an exciting race and - at the end - a deserved first Grand Prix win for the quiet Ulsterman John Watson and the American Penske team.

Reutemann was setting some sort of record for first-lap retirements, this time with clutch trouble, and the best Brabham performance was by the girl driver, Lella Lombardi, in one of the cars entered by RAM Racing. She was placed twelfth. Loris Kessel, in the other RAM Brabham, was running at the finish but was unclassified, being ten laps behind the winner.

Ferrari were back for the European Grand Prix in The Netherlands and it proved a great race, Hunt (Marlboro–McLaren) winning from Regazzoni (Ferrari) and Andretti (John Player Special), but for Brabham matters were going from bad to worse. Pace went out on Lap 53 with an oil leak. Reutemann on Lap 11 with clutch trouble.

Still badly scarred, Lauda made a remarkable comeback in the Italian Grand Prix and finished fourth to Ronnie Peterson (March–Ford). his team-mate Regazzoni and Jacques Laffite (Ligier–Matra).

Ferrari's entered a third car and there was some public surprise when the driver turned out to be, not some local daredevil entered to please the Italian *aficionados* but Brabham's No. 1, Carlos Reutemann.

Those on the inside of the sport were not so surprised. Lolé's disenchantment with Brabham had been pretty obvious all season and he had been seen on a number of occasions in close conference with other team owners or managers. Meanwhile, his recent performances had been such that Ecclestone & Co. were not to be seen weeping at his somewhat sudden departure. Stommelen, who had acquited himself so well in Germany, took over BT45/1 while Pace, who had been the best 'Carlos' all season, had BT45/3, still with the new brakes, although modified in a bid to prevent the fluid boiling as it had in Austria.

There was some satisfaction for the Brabham team when Pace circulated faster in practice than Reutemann in his Ferrari but, sadly, there was to be no more. Stommelen's engine blew and in the race itself Pace dropped out with piston failure after only four laps. Stommelen did manage 41 laps but then further engine trouble ended his race.

6

'THE OTHER CARLOS'

There are racing-drivers who have proven their greatness beyond doubt – Fangio, Moss, Brabham, Clark, Hill, Rindt, Lauda ... There are others whose potential can only be a matter of conjecture, men who had a hint of greatness about them but whose careers were tragically cut short before that potential could be realised ... One of the finest of these was Carlos 'Moco' Pace, 'the other Carlos' as he was known to distinguish him from Carlos Reutemann.

After the departure of Reutemann to the Ferrari team and Stommelen's last-minute substitution, there were still three races to go to complete the 1976 Grand Prix season. The Brabham team had no intention of writing the season off as a dead loss even at this late stage of the game and they looked around for a replacement for the moody Argentinian, a back-up man for Moco.

A fellow named Larry Perkins had had a few outings with the struggling Boro-Ensign team and his efforts in an outclassed car had caught the attention of the Brabham management. They signed him for the rest of the season, doubtless hoping that a little of that Australian magic might rub off.

The bespectacled 26-year-old Aussie was one of four racing-driver brothers, born and reared on the family cattle station at Cowangie, population 10 – a younger Chips Rafferty transferred from the celluloid screen to the excitement of the race track. Larry was the winner of the 1971 Australian 'Driver for Europe' Award; did well with GRD and Brabham in Formula Three in 1973; spent a year working on Chris Amon's Formula One project; then won the European Formula Three Championship in 1975 with Ralt RT1, built for him by Ron Tauranac. His handful of 1976 drives with the Ensign car, designed by Mo Nunn but entered by a Dutch brewing company, had impressed other people in addition to Brabham.

For the Canadian Grand Prix, Perkins had BT45/3 with wishbone rear suspension and yet another version of the SPICA fuel injection equipment. Carlos Pace had a completely new car, BT45/5, which was some six kilogrammes lighter than its immediate predecessors. In practice new airbox and engine-cover arrangements were tried but eventually discarded as spoiling the airflow.

Larry Perkins had an unlucky start with the team, his engine blowing up during the practice sessions, and he switched to BT45/1.

It proved another good race with no less than eight drivers – James Hunt (the winner), Depailler, Andretti, Scheckter, Mass, Regazzoni, Brabham's No. 1, Carlos Pace, and Lauda – all on the same lap at the finish. The rookie Perkins was seventeenth, two laps behind the leaders, but for the Brabham team it was a pleasure to have two cars start and two finish a race, even though neither had finished in a points-scoring position.

For the moment, at least, Brabham were content to take their satisfaction one race at a time. Which was perhaps just as well . . .

It was short-lived satisfaction which was typical of this frustrating season for the team. In the United States Grand Prix, Perkins had trouble with his front suspension and retired on Lap 30 and the following lap saw Moco follow him into the dead car park after a collision with Mass.

Truth to tell, no one was greatly worried about the Brabhams, apart from Brabham, that is, since all eyes were on the Hunt versus Lauda battle for the Championship. Hunt was the winner at Watkins Glen with Lauda third and everything rested on the last race of the season in Japan.

Japan is a long way away and Brabham decided to cut their losses a little, taking only two cars instead of three, neither of them being fitted with the experimental braking system. It was to be a dismal end to a disappointing season. In appalling weather conditions of rain and mist in which both Pace and Perkins 'lost it' and spun, both Brabham drivers withdrew; Emerson Fittipaldi did likewise; and so did Lauda.

Andretti won but Hunt's third place was sufficient to give him the Championship by one point. Pace was a lowly fourteenth. Ferrari won the Constructors' award and Brabham were a sad ninth.

No less than fifty-eight drivers had taken part in Championship races during the year, a remarkable number. Pace was one of only five drivers to start in all eighteen races, Brambilla, Hunt, Tom Pryce and Scheckter being the others.

For 1977, Gordon Murray produced the BT45B although the team

One of the most successful of Brabham 'works' drivers
was the Argentinian, Carlos Reutemann, but the enigmatic
'Lolé' never quite made it to the World Championship.

Brazil's Carlos Pace and Reutemann made a powerful duo
but 'Moco's' death in a plane crash robbed Grand Prix
racing of a man Bernie Ecclestone feels was destined for
greatness.

started the season still running the BT45s. The cars were again powered by the Alfa-Romeo 115-12 engine, the team continuing under Martini sponsorship. Pace was the No. 1 driver and when Roger Penske announced his team's withdrawal from the Grand Prix scene, Bernie Ecclestone nipped in smartly to sign John Watson as Pace's partner.

Moco looked forward to the season with confidence and assured all and sundry that the team would soon be winning races. A decision had finally been taken in favour of the Lucas fuel injection system, Alfa-Romeo had worked hard on engine development during the off-season and all looked well.

The first race of the new season – the Argentine Grand Prix – did little to dispel that aura of confidence. Watson, first time out in the car, qualified on the front row next to World Champion James Hunt. He led the race until his tyres gave trouble and took the lead again when Hunt retired. Unfortunately, on Lap 41 the gearbox mounting studs sheared, the back end of the car started to flap around and the Bognor-based Irishman also had to retire.

Pace, meanwhile, was going well and eventually took the lead, but the killing heat began to affect him – the Brabham cockpit ventilation, or lack of it, didn't help too much – and he slowed sufficiently for Jody Scheckter to catch and pass him, gaining a victory for the Wolf first time out. Only five cars finished and Pace collapsed after crossing the finishing-line.

The circus moved on to Brazil but there was no escape from the heat and its attendant problems. Pace took an early lead, but with the glare of the sun full in his eyes went into a slide and collided with Hunt's McLaren. Limping into the pits for repairs, the Brazilian knew that his chance of repeating his 1976 win had gone.

Another 'coming together' put paid to Watson on Lap 30 and a familiar 1976 story was repeated. But it was early days yet and with Pace and the team both lying third in their respective championships it was off to South Africa where Lauda was to win in a race marred by a shocking accident.

The Shadows up-and-coming British driver Tom Pryce was killed when a couple of over-eager marshals ran across the track. Pryce could not avoid the second of the two, who was carrying a heavy fire-extinguisher, and the driver was killed instantly by the extinguisher which hit him with all the velocity of a shell.

The Brabhams had better fortune. Watson earned a Championship point in sixth place – he was only 20 seconds behind the winner – whilst Pace, two laps adrift, was thirteenth.

Thirteenth. For the superstitious – and there are many of them in motor sport – it was an omen.

Pace went home to Brazil to enjoy a short break before the ardours of the rest of the season. It was there that he died, killed in a light aircraft crash. He left a widow and two children.

It was a loss to the sport – he had always given of his best – but the loss to the Brabham team was incalculable. Pace had persevered when Reutemann gave up and because he spoke fluent Italian he had been the perfect link with Alfa-Romeo. The testing he had done in 1976 had paid off but now much of the knowledge had gone with him and in many respects it would mean the team starting all over again. To all intents and purposes, it was the end of Brabham's South American period.

Would Moco have ever been World Champion? Who can tell? Brazil has produced two world motor-racing champions, Emerson Fittipaldi and Nelson Piquet. Many of the experts predict that there will soon be another – Ayrton Senna. Should there have been a fourth – Carlos Pace? The signs were there. If he could have had just one season with a car running on top form throughout he could have made it. But we shall never know . . .

7

THE AUSTRIAN CONNECTION

It sounds like a novel, but it is a true story. There was a man they called 'The King of the Mountains'. He married. But in a war-torn Europe under Hitler's domination, the fact that his wife was not pure Aryan was held against him and they both suffered persecution. This then was the unlikely background to the Brabham team's search for a replacement for the ill-starred Carlos Pace.

The man they called 'The King of the Mountains' was an Austrian named Hans Stuck, born in 1900, who became a racing-driver when in his twenties. In those days hill climbs were major events and Stuck, driving first Austro-Daimlers and then Mercedes, soon became the champion hill-climb driver of Europe, 'The King of the Mountains'.

In 1934, Stuck joined the German Auto Union Grand Prix team, winning three Grands Prix in his initial season (including the first Swiss Grand Prix) and one the next, whilst continuing to dominate the hill-climb world.

After the miseries of the Second World War, Hans returned to the race circuits and, in 1950, driving a Formula Two AFM, defeated the great Ascari in the Monza Grand Prix (and Ascari was driving a Ferrari!).

Stuck resumed hill climbing and in 1960, at the age of sixty, won his last German Mountain Championship, although he did not finally retire from competitive motoring until he was an OAP – at sixty-five.

Stuck's son, Hans-Joachim, born in Munich, took on his father's mantle, flinging BMWs up the mountains in much the style of Stuck Senior. On the race circuits, Hans-Joachim, although his Grand Prix career had been a mixed one so far, had earned a reputation as a sound 'wet weather' driver.

Hans-Joachim Stuck had had a couple of seasons with the March team and was being sought by the German ATS team. In the event, they would have to wait until 1979 before getting him from the Shadows team. For this season at least, his destiny was elsewhere . . .

Following the death of Pace, it was to Hans-Joachim that Brabham now turned and he joined the team in time to take part in the United States Grand Prix West at Long Beach. They had three cars for the race, all now fitted to BT45B specification with a modified rear end.

Stuck made a promising first appearance, completing 53 laps before being forced to retire with brake trouble. His team-mate, John Watson, met trouble of every sort imaginable ... plus one or two fiction-writers would have hesitated to use.

First of all, James Hunt's car literally ran over Watson's. Watson kept going but the collision had caused tyre damage and he had to go into the pits. Back on the circuit, he started to work his way through the field, an art at which he is an accomplished master, when his engine died. Mechanics came out to the car and found nothing wrong – the hapless Watson had inadvertently knocked off the cut-out switch. Back on the track again, he was black-flagged by the marshals for receiving outside assistance.

The laurels went to Mario Andretti in his John Player Special, the little Italian-American's victory being popular with the home crowd. Andretti won again in Spain where Stuck drove his Brabham into sixth place. Gordon Murray had made a number of changes including new cooling ducts for the brakes. The gearbox had also been modified. Unfortunately, it was the fuel metering unit that played up on Watson's car and forced him to retire on Lap 64 when he was lying fifth.

The team took off for some testing in Italy at Bolocco, Alfa's own test track, prior to Monaco. It seemed to pay off. The cars ran well in practice using a new rear aerofoil. Stuck was fastest in the first practice session and eventually Watson secured pole position. So far so good ...

Came race day. An electrical fault on Lap 19 caused a cockpit fire and Hans Stuck hastily baled out. Watson was scrapping for the lead nearly all the way, but his race was run when the gearbox seized on Lap 48, leaving that well-known resident of Monte Carlo, Mr Jody Scheckter, to go on and win in his Wolf.

Watson won the pole again for the Belgian Grand Prix and shot into the lead right away, but Andretti ran into him from behind and that was that, much to John's disgust. Stuck kept at it, however, and gained another sixth place, a lap behind the winner, Gunnar Nilsson (JPS-Ford), who was later to die so tragically of cancer.

The Irishman was again on the front row for the Swedish Grand Prix and was second until involved in Scheckter's spin-off. This time he

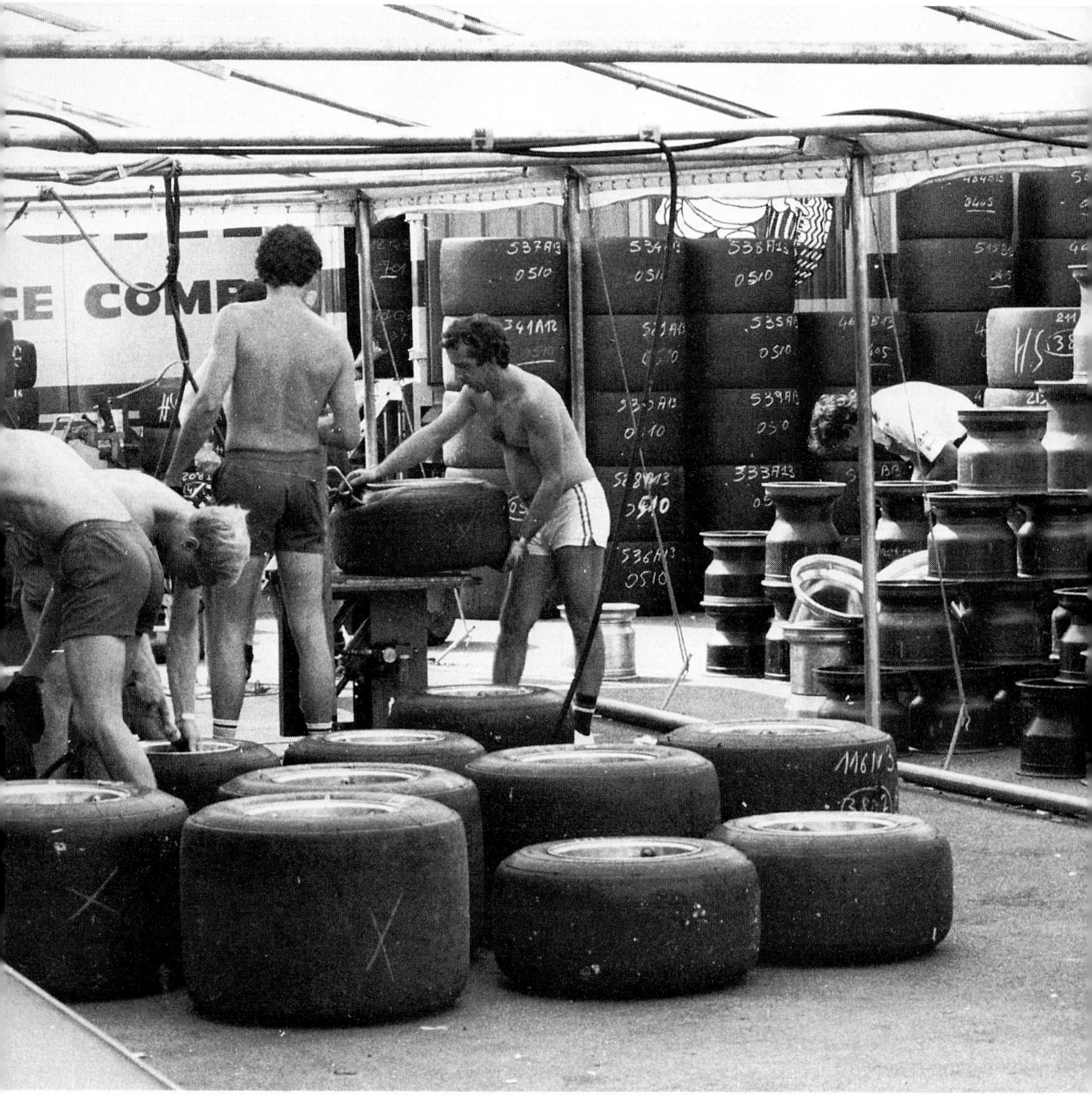

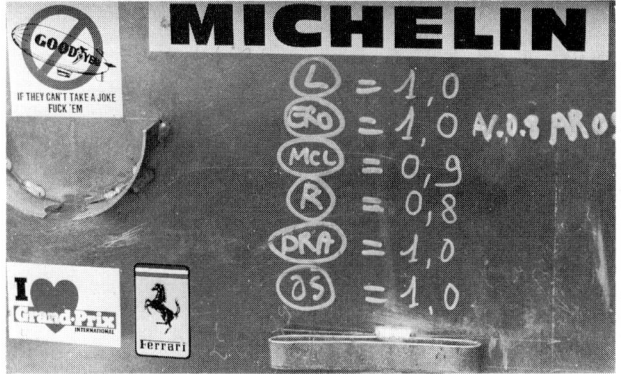

Just a glimpse of the tyres and wheels required for one Grand Prix race today. And this 'tyre corner' is just Michelin's alone.

The tyre boys have to keep a careful check on their individual customers – Brabham, McLaren, Ligier and Renault among those listed here – but they also have a rude message for the competition.

managed to keep going and finished fifth to Laffite (Ligier), Mass (McLaren), Reutemann (Ferrari) and Depailler (Tyrrell). Stuck again finished a lap behind the winner – in tenth place.

If Watson thought he had had bad luck so far it was just as well he could not see into the future, for worse lay in store at the French Grand Prix. He led nearly all the way, but just 30 seconds from the finish his Brabham–Alfa ran out of fuel and a surprised and grateful Mario Andretti (JPS) swept past to win by almost the narrowest of margins – just $1\frac{1}{2}$ seconds.

Watson, alas, paid the penalty of the weight of the BT45B, the thirstiness of the Alfa engine and the temperature, which soared to 106 degrees Fahrenheit! Before the race, and employing the heaviest consumption figures shown in practice, the mechanics had calculated how much fuel would be needed to complete the distance, and added three extra gallons for good luck. It wasn't enough. Presumably, the heat and evaporation had taken care of the rest.

Meanwhile, Stuck in the second Brabham, had to retire on Lap 64 after a collision with Laffite's Ligier had damaged the Brabham's air-starter.

There was more bad luck to come in the British Grand Prix at Silverstone. Watson took the lead at the start and looked a certain winner until troubled by fuel pressure problems; James Hunt, who had been in a bad spell himself, going on to gain a first victory for the McLaren M26. There was some consolation for the Brabham team in that Stuck drove the second car to a commendable fifth place, not much over a minute behind the winner.

Two events which attracted little enough attention at the time but which were to alter the face of motor racing occurred at that Silverstone Grand Prix. The first Formula One radial tyres and the first turbo of the modern generation of racing cars (there had been an experimental Rover–BRM turbo earlier) made their debut. The tyres were Michelin radials and they were fitted to the lone experimental Renault turbo.

By 1984, all Grand Prix teams – bar one – would be running turbos and Jody Scheckter, Nelson Piquet and Niki Lauda would have won the world title on Michelin radials.

John Watson was taking matters philosophically, which was just as well. He again started on the front row for the German Grand Prix, chased Scheckter for the lead over the first eight laps then blew up in a big way. Again there was some consolation – Stuck drove well to finish third and was only thwarted from making a late challenge by fear of running out of fuel. As Watson had done in the French Grand Prix, Hans-Joachim wondered if he was going to run dry on the last lap but the Brabham just struggled over the line, an effort which naturally went down well with the German crowd.

Stuck now moved up to eleventh in the table, Watson being tenth; and the team fifth in the Constructors' Championship.

At least Watson finished the Austrian Grand Prix, but most of the race he was near to last and it was Stuck, once more finishing third (this time to Jones and Lauda), who kept the Brabham flag flying. For once, Watson had been depressed before the start. In trying both his own car and the spare he had been singularly unimpressed with the handling of both. There had also been the usual problem of the car's weight and fuel requirements, Watson deciding to run on hard tyres, a decision with which Stuck was inclined to agree.

When Watson found himself lapped by his team-mate, he got a move on, caught up the field and posted the fastest lap. It was all a little late, there being only one lap to go, but it did put the Irishman into eighth place and raise the question of what might have been had Watson himself felt happier about the car at the start. Stuck moved up two places in the Drivers' Championship as a result of this race and was looking pretty good.

The Grand Prix circus moved on to The Netherlands and Round Thirteen of the Championship. Not surprisingly, Watson's ill fortune continued. Forced over a kerb on the first lap, the car's sump was holed and his race was soon run. Stuck was a little disappointing after his recent form and finished seventh. He was, perhaps, not unmindful that the grapevine was buzzing with the rumour that the great Niki Lauda would vacate his Ferrari seat to join Brabham next season. There are always rumours in the tight little world of Grand Prix racing – this one had the ring of truth.

The Italian Grand Prix was another write-off for Martini-Brabham, doubly disappointing in view of the team's Italian sponsor. Sponsors put up a lot of money and they do expect results. Watson's fatal attraction for kerbs continued. This time he hit one with such force that an engine mounting broke. Stuck lasted 31 laps before his engine expired.

Hans-Joachim qualified on the front row of the grid at Watkins Glen, led the race until Lap 15 and then went off the road when his clutchless car jumped out of gear going into a corner. Most of the drivers elected to drive on wet tyres in view of the weather prospects. Watson gambled on a drying circuit, paid the penalty and lost valuable time in the pits changing to 'wets' – his twelfth place was good for neither driver nor owner.

The dismal story continued in Canada. Watson, in collision with Ronnie Peterson, went out on the first lap. Stuck lasted just nineteen laps before, once again, his engine 'conked out'.

So to Japan and the final round. Lauda, assured of the World Championship, had not raced in Canada, much to Ferrari's annoyance, and he was not even present at Fuji.

It wasn't very good PR for the Grand Prix circus with organisers and spectators far from pleased. Whatever his reasons, Hunt also raised a few eyebrows when, after leading from start to finish, he rushed away from the circuit without taking his trophy, posing for pictures, and so on.

Folk could be forgiven for wondering if some drivers were forgetting 'Joe Public', but the Brabham team were probably relieved that the arguments over Lauda and Hunt obscured a seventh place for Stuck and retirement on Lap 29 for Watson (gearbox trouble).

'Dame Rumour' turned out to be correct. Lauda joined Brabham for 1978, Watson stayed with the team and Stuck moved to the Shadows team. Yet the biggest sensation to come from the Brabham camp would be provided by Gordon Murray. For the moment that design was still on the drawing-board and in the fertile brain of the brilliant Brabham designer.

Brabham started the season with two new cars, 'C' versions of the BT45. The main alteration was a lower nose section to allow more air to get to the front tyres and ease the overheating problems which had occurred in hot weather the previous season. There was a tubular-mounted rear-wing assembly, the tubes being used to carry air and the rear fire-extinguisher bottles. These were the cars which Brabham took to Argentina for the first round of the World Championship and a season which would see the revival of the tyre war, Goodyear versus Michelin.

Mario Andretti (JPS) was the winner, chased for most of the way by both Brabhams. A water leak caused Watson's engine to blow up with three-quarters of the race completed but Lauda moved up into second

Niki Lauda at speed in the Brabham–Alfa BT48, a car with a unique profile which in some ways was a throwback to the pre-cigar tube days.

From 1976 to 1978, the Brabham profile was vastly different from the 1979 BT46. The reason? Mainly due to a 'flat' Alfa engine being used in the earlier years compared to the V–12 of 1979.

place and stayed there until the finish despite a strong challenge from Depailler (Tyrrell).

In practice for the Brazilian race, Lauda tried the old nose section and found the car appreciably faster. An SOS was sent to England for an old-type nose for Watson's car and just after the Sunday 'warm up' a chopper landed by the pits with the precious nose section aboard. Just the same, the race ended as a South American bonanza. Reutemann, in his Ferrari, won the race for the third time with Emerson Fittipaldi (Fittipaldi–Ford) second, a rare moment of satisfaction for the Brazilian Copersucar outfit. Lauda was third, however, with Watson just out of the points in seventh place.

Two races gone – Brabham were second in the Constructors', second in the Drivers'. Things appeared to be looking up.

Equipped with new-design Goodyears for the South African Grand Prix, Lauda's BT46 soon collected pole position, but in the race itself, the engine blew on Lap 52. It was Watson's turn and but for spinning on an oil slick he might have won. As it was he took third place behind Peterson (JPS) and Depailler (Tyrrell).

The original BT46 was the spare for the United States Grand Prix West, the cars that had been used in South African and now in the USA having some 69 changes, according to the designer. These included new skirts, a bigger oil radiator with revised mounting, an altered fuel and brake system and a new nose shape. The changes availed the team nothing – Watson's race ending following an oil tank explosion on Lap 9 and Lauda's with ignition failure on Lap 27. Reutemann won again and the former Brabham driver looked a hot tip for the title.

Ahead was Monaco – and another change of fortune . . .

Reutemann gained the pole position but made a poor start and was virtually put of contention when he lost a lap through a puncture suffered when Lauda's Brabham came too close. In the other Brabham John Watson was away to a terrific start, but constantly harried by the Tyrrell driver, Patrick Depailler, he began to have braking problems and went down the escape road at the chicane. With Depailler now in first place, Lauda took up the chase but thirty laps from the end, the Austrian pitted for a new tyre. That appeared to be that but Lauda, rejoining the race in sixth position, stormed through the field, breaking the lap record in the process, to regain second place. Depailler held on for his first Grand Prix win – the wine flowed and France celebrated *en masse* that night – but with Lauda second and Watson fourth, Brabham fortunes were on the up-turn. Lauda was now fourth in the Drivers' Championship with Watson sixth. The marque was third to Lotus and Tyrrell.

Belgium was a slap in the face for the Brabham team. Lauda didn't complete a lap after colliding with Scheckter at the start, whilst Watson retired on Lap 16 with by now familiar damage resulting from hitting a kerb following a spin.

Lauda's luck was not much better in Spain, engine trouble forcing his retirement after 56 laps, but Watson was fifth, just over a minute behind the winner, Mario Andretti (JPS–Lotus).

The Swedish Grand Prix, thanks to the ingenious imagination of designer Gordon Murray, saw Brabham's first victory in almost three years – but, oh, what a storm it caused.

The Brabham team arrived at the Swedish circuit with two BT46 cars both fitted with a big fan at the rear and tight skirting on the chassis. The fans were, temporarily, covered with dustbin lids and were accordingly treated with disrespect by most of the teams, with 'loads of old rubbish' being typical of the remarks made.

But when the dustbin lids were taken off, the cars were wheeled out and Watson and Lauda got on the first and second rows of the grid respectively, rival teams began to think again. Some thought the devices were an infringement of the regulations, others that they were dangerous, some were just annoyed because Murray had thought of it first.

The basic argument was whether or not the fan was intended to cool the engine or to create an aerodynamic advantage by 'sucking' the rear-end of the car tight to the track. Some of the drivers were more concerned about the dangers resulting from the fans picking up stones and other debris and 'throwing' them back at following cars. 'Forget the politics and the legal bull,' snapped Mario Andretti, 'it's got to be stopped for safety reasons.'

Andretti's entrant, Colin Chapman, joined by Ken Tyrrell, John Surtees and Teddy Mayer (McLaren) put in a protest but it was rejected.

Lauda had a decisive win (Watson went out on Lap 19) and, whatever the rights and wrongs of the argument, there was no doubt that it was a remarkable achievement for Gordon Murray & Co. to win with such a revolutionary car *the first time out*. The Alfa-Romeo mechanics with the Brabham team were in tears – after all they hadn't handled a Grand Prix winner since 1951.

Before the French Grand Prix, the fan car had been banned, but the Swedish result was allowed to stand as the cars had raced there with official approval. The ban meant wholesale changes in the BT46 for the French race. The monocoque was about the only thing retained – cooling system, bodywork, front and rear suspension, all had to be changed.

Despite this, Watson took the pole with a defiant, 'That will show them we don't need a fan to do well', and followed up with fourth place in the race behind Andretti, Peterson and Hunt. Lauda retired with a sick engine after 10 laps.

Reutemann, on his best form, was the victor at Brands Hatch, but Lauda was breathing down his exhaust-pipe, with Watson not far away third.

Andretti was back in the winner's circle after the German Grand Prix and the Lotus grip was beginning to tighten on both championships. Watson was just out of the points in seventh place, whilst engine trouble put paid to Lauda after eleven laps.

It was back to 'two races in one' in Austria: seven laps on 'slicks' before the rains came down, then 47 laps on 'wets' with four of the original starters missing. Andretti being a 'first race' casualty, it was left to his team-mate, Ronnie Peterson, to win the race proper. Watson was seventh, a lap behind, but Lauda bent his car on Lap 28.

The Chapman stable again demonstrated its superiority in Holland with Andretti and Peterson first and second, but there was no doubt that the Brabhams were the best of the opposition, Lauda and Watson being third and fourth.

Round Fourteen of the Championship in Italy was the craziest and unfortunately, the most tragic of the season. Mario Andretti gained a well-earned World Championship, but his triumph was muted by the death in hospital next day of his team-mate, Ronnie Peterson, injured in a ten-car accident, which climaxed a chaotic start and was prelude to a chaotic finish.

Andretti and Villeneuve were the first two home but both were penalised one minute for jumping the start and that time burden dropped them in the official standings from first and second to sixth and seventh. Lauda was declared the official winner with team-mate Watson runner-up. Nevertheless, the revised standings did not prevent Andretti from taking the title.

Both Bernie Ecclestone and Gordon Murray, however, were looking beyond the winner's rostrum. Shrewd observers as they are, both had made a mental note of a young Brazilian driver, one Nelson Piquet, who had driven in promising style despite the handicap of a somewhat decrepit McLaren M23.

The artificial victory of Monza, welcome though it was, was virtually season's end for the Brabham team, neither Lauda nor Watson finishing at Watkins Glen or Montreal. Not that the French-Canadian city cared with a French-Canadian driver, Gilles Villeneuve, winning their inaugural Grand Prix.

The 'fan car' having been barred, work naturally ceased on BT47, the projected 'fan car' for the 1979 season, and the BT48 came into being.

The BT48 was powered by an engine evolved by Carlo Chiti in order to meet the requirements of 'ground effect' chassis, the powerful but wide flat-12 being unsuited for this purpose. Ferrari, committed to a flat-12 had tremendous troubles, but for Brabham, Chiti produced a 60-degree V-12 of 2991 cc which, although using many flat-12 parts, allowed for underwing airflow and made Gordon Murray happy in this respect.

Murray and Chiti got along well which, under the circumstances, was for the best since, although the V-12 was suitable for 'ground effect' aerodynamics, there were plenty of other problems concerning the engine, resulting in trouble from the start.

It was probably a happy release when, at the end of the 1979 season, Alfa-Romeo decided to build their own Formula One car with, of course, an Alfa engine, and Brabham opted to go back to Cosworth power, 'such sweet thunder', as writer John Blunsden once described it.

Lauda was back with the team as No. 1 driver but Watson had moved to Marlboro-McLaren and Nelson Piquet, who had caught the eye the previous season, moved into the Irishman's seat.

The wheeler-dealings of the off-season had brought a change of sponsorship too. Martini had moved across to sponsor Lotus, replacing John Player Special, but Bernie Ecclestone had another Italian backer, the giant Parmalat dairy combine.

A man who played a big part behind the scenes during this period was David Yorke, one of the most successful racing managers of all time. Yorke had been in motor racing a long time, managing Peter Whitehead and his Ferrari back in 1950. Millionaire Tony Vandervell took him on and he managed the Vanwall team in those years when they were putting Great Britain on the Grand Prix map. He had another very successful period as manager of John Wyer's conquering long-distance team of GT40 Fords.

When the Italian Tecno organisation decided to enter Grand Prix racing with the backing of the Martini drinks firm, it was to David Yorke that they turned for guidance. But the Tecno belongs amongst the lost causes of motor racing and soon disappeared from the scene. Martini, however, asked Yorke to stay and look after their motor-racing interests with the result that he and they joined forces with Brabham in the mid-seventies.

When Martini moved to Lotus, Yorke's association with Brabham continued and he was the guest of the team when he died peacefully in his sleep on 17th August, 1984, the night after the first practice for the Austrian Grand Prix. He was seventy.

New Zealand's gift to motor-sport journalism, Eoin Young, tells a delightful story about the time when the prototype Porsche 917 was giving handling problems. Scorning the computers, electronic scanners, wind-tunnel tests and even blueprints without which most modern designers and team managers would not move an inch, David Yorke merely instructed the mechanics to chop off the long tail 'and see if it helps'.

The death of David Yorke was not only a loss to the Brabham team but to motor racing in general. That, fortunately, was still years ahead when the first Parmalat-sponsored season opened with the Argentine Grand Prix in January 1979.

The Brabham team arrived with a BT48 for Lauda and a BT46 for Piquet. Lauda soon had trouble with the fuel-injection system on the new Alfa engine and with the side skirts on the chassis, these failing to provide an effective 'seal' with the ground. Lauda took out the older car in order to qualify then went back to wrestling with the problems of the BT48.

It was hardly a propitious start to the new season. Worse was to come when the race got under way, an eight-car pile-up at the start eliminating five of the entrants. Piquet's first 'works' drive came to an abrupt end as he was dragged from the wreckage of the BT46 by Arturo Merzario and his own team-mate, Niki Lauda. John Watson was officially blamed for the débâcle and heavily fined, a decision which was to aggravate the already strained relationship between the authorities and the Formula One Constructors' Association.

Lauda's Brabham was amongst the cars in a depleted field when the race re-started – but not for long. On Lap 8, Lauda retired from the fray with fuel-pressure problems and Laffite, in one of the Ligier–Fords, went on to score a victory for France.

Brabham had one thing to be grateful for – Piquet suffered only sprained toes as a result of being trapped by the feet. Had the car caught fire it is extremely unlikely that his fellow-drivers would have been able to get him out.

Despite the handicap of his injuries, the plucky Piquet qualified a new BT48 for the Brazilian race and Lauda did likewise, the skirt and fuel problems having been ironed out. Gear selection hampered by flexing linkage came up as a new problem for Lauda, and Piquet ran into Regazzoni's Williams when a sudden stab of pain in his injured foot caused him to take his foot off the brake pedal.

The tough, one-time Rugby-playing Guy Ligier must have thought that Christmas had come as Laffite again got the chequered flag, followed home by his partner, Depailler.

The South African Grand Prix ran for two laps before the rains came. Four drivers re-started on 'slicks' instead of wet tyres and their gamble saved them some pit-stops. Piquet was one of the four but he faded towards the finish and could do no better than seventh, Lauda being sixth. For the Ligiers it was back to bread-and-margarine, both cars failing to finish, one spinning on 'slicks', the other suffering a puncture.

There was little joy for Paramalat-Brabham at the United States Grand Prix West as the Ferraris resumed their winning ways. Tambay's McLaren slid into the back of Lauda's car on the first lap and put both of them out of the race. Piquet was eighth out of nine classified finishers, two laps adrift.

Ligier won again in Spain, Lauda lasting 63 laps before going out with a water leak; Piquet only 15 – broken fuel-metering unit.

In Belgium both cars went on Lap 23 with engine trouble and at Monaco, Piquet's drive-shaft broke on Lap 68. Lauda was unlucky in the Principality – in third place on Lap 21, he was rammed by Didier Pironi (Tyrrell) who had already wreaked considerable mayhem on the rest of the field. Only six cars were classed as finishers.

The sad story continued in the French Grand Prix. Lauda spun on Lap 23 and was unable to re-start; Piquet was up with the leaders but went off the road on Lap 54. His car had been showing signs of oversteer for some time.

The British Grand Prix was held at Silverstone that year but it might as well have been in Disneyland for all the good it did Brabham. Piquet spun on the first lap and could not re-start, Lauda lasted only twelve laps before fading brakes ended his race.

At this point, things were so bad that it was almost a matter for celebration when Piquet was classified last of the twelve finishers in Germany, Lauda having engine trouble on Lap 27.

Austria was worse, neither car finishing.

One advantage about being on the floor, as a certain heavyweight once remarked, is that the only way to go is up. The Dutch Grand Prix gave some weight to that assertion since although Lauda, who had an injured wrist, withdrew after four laps, Piquet, driving the spare after his car developed an oil leak in practice, finished fourth behind Alan Jones (Williams), Jody Scheckter (Ferrari) and Laffite (Ligier).

At Monza, Piquet's car was wrecked in an early collision with Regazzoni but Lauda finished fourth this time, the first occasion on which he had finished a race since South Africa. But already there were rumours that the Austrian fancied a McLaren drive again and would not be a Brabham man much longer.

Like so many rumours there was a half-truth in it somewhere. Bernie Ecclestone had offered Lauda a good deal for the next season; Bernie, Gordon Murray and Parmalat had agreed that the time had come to drop the unsuccessful Alfa engine and join the majority with Ford-Cosworth; and Gordon and the Brabham mechanics had been working flat out to produce three brand-new Parmalat-Brabham-Fords for the Canadian Grand Prix on 30 September. So they weren't too happy when on the Friday before the race – after driving the new car for just one lap – Lauda announced his retirement from Grand Prix racing, *effective immediately*. 'My heart is not in it any more', he said.

So there was the Brabham team with three new BT49s and only one driver, Nelson Piquet. An SOS was sent out over the public address system for 30-year-old Argentinian Ricardo Zunino, a saloon-car driver in his homeland who had shown promise in single-seaters since racing in Europe.

Wearing Lauda's overalls and helmet, Zunino drove well. His seventh place was quite an achievement after an enforced stop to repair a broken gear link. Piquet did even better and looked to have a firm grip on third place when his gearbox broke just a few laps from the finish.

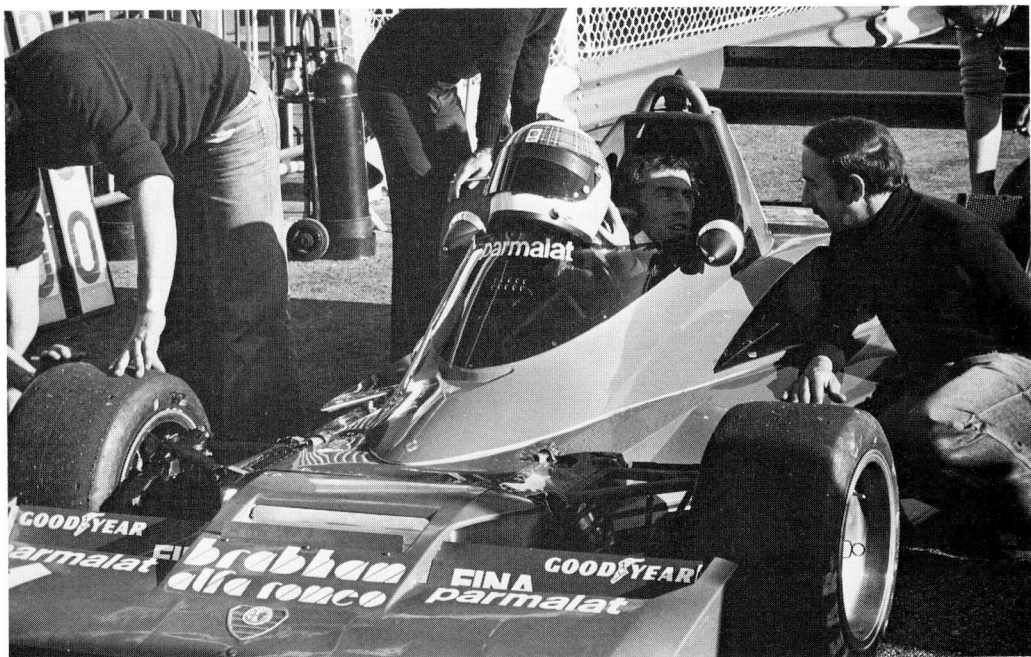

Another World Champion, Jackie Stewart, tries out a Brabham–Alfa for size. 'What do you think of it?' ask the pit crew.

'What are they going to tell me now?' World Champion Niki Lauda looks quizzically from beneath his helmet while the pit crew confer.

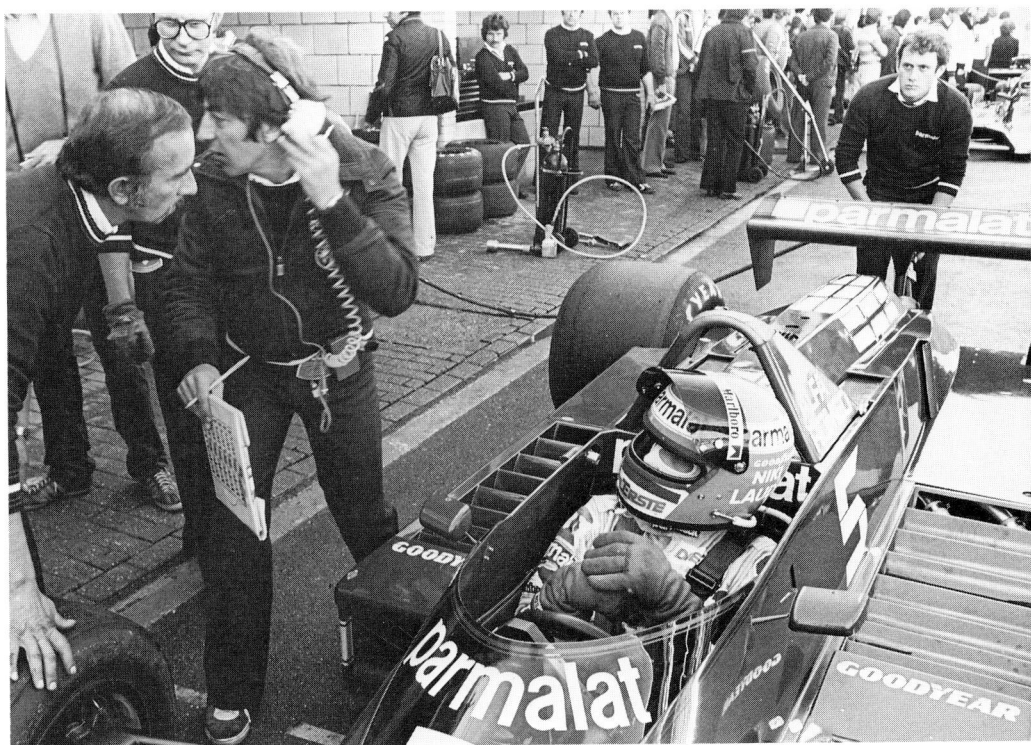

The new cars had the old front and rear suspension but everything else about them was new. The former normal weight of the Alfa-powered cars had been reduced by 40 pounds and, of course, in race conditions the difference would be even more marked, since the Ford engine would not drink so much.

The fifteenth and final round of the Championship was at Watkins Glen. Piquet recorded the fastest lap but a broken drive-shaft put him out on Lap 53, Zunino's race ended with a Lap 25 accident.

At least the season ended on a more hopeful note than seemed possible for Brabham at one stage. The BT49 looked a contender, the Ford engine was a proven winner (125 Grands Prix so far) and in Nelson Piquet, the team had a driver whose best days were ahead of him rather than behind.

No designer who wants to win can rest on his laurels. For the new season Murray revised the aerodynamics and the bodywork and designed a completely new rear suspension. In testing at the Paul Ricard circuit in France, Piquet put up some very fast times. The team was in good heart when it arrived in Buenos Aires for the first Grand Prix of the 1980 season. There were three BT49s, resplendent in blue-and-white livery, for Piquet and Zunino. One was the car which Piquet had driven at Watkins Glen, the other two were brand new. They seemed to be as fast as any of the opposition and Piquet got off to a good start in the Championship by finishing second to Jones (Williams). It was the Australian's fifth win in seven races.

In Brazil, the Brabhams did not go too well and René Arnoux (Renault) gained the first Grand Prix victory of his career, a win he was to repeat in South Africa.

Turbo-charged engines were coming into fashion and were obviously going to be a major threat to the normally-aspirated engines except, perhaps, on twisty circuits like Monaco and Long Beach. Long Beach was next on the programme. Would it see the turbos beaten?

Nelson Piquet, who had picked up three points in South Africa, was third to Arnoux and Jones in the Championship and, yes, the pundits were right – Long Beach did give the 'normals' a chance. Piquet notched-up a most impressive win and ended one of the longest losing runs in Brabham's proud history. He was now tied with Arnoux for the Drivers' Championship and Brabham were locked with Renault for the Constructors' Championship.

Gordon Murray was optimistic about chances at Zolder, first European race of the season: 'Historically, we have been quick at Zolder. It is a handling and braking circuit and we appear to be good in both those departments.'

Alas, Piquet went off and Pironi (Ligier) won the Belgian Grand Prix! Fortunately, Piquet was undamaged and his car only slightly so. Murray still had high hopes when the circus moved on to Monte Carlo: 'Nelson professes not to like road circuits but after Long Beach I wonder.'

Murray's belief in the driver was justified, Piquet gaining third place in Monaco to take over the lead in the title race, a point ahead of Arnoux and three ahead of Jones.

For the Spanish Grand Prix, the BT49s were fitted with Hewland gearboxes instead of the Weismanns - 'rested' for further checks. The cars went straight from Monaco for testing which Murray hoped would make them competitive on a circuit where they had not acquitted themselves well in the past.

FISA, the international sporting federation, and FOCA, the Formula One Constructors' Association, locked in one of their periodic battles over the Spanish Grand Prix and although in the end it was run, the official body declared that points earned would not count for the Championships. This was rough luck on winner Alan Jones but an 'ill-wind' insofar as Piquet was concerned, since it left him top of the table.

Before the French Grand Prix, Brabham went to Silverstone for the day, it being a circuit not dissimilar to Paul Ricard where the French race was to be run. Piquet put in a lap at 1 minute, 10.6 seconds, faster than Alan Jones's pole-qualifying time the year before. But Jones had the last laugh by winning the race itself. Piquet finished fourth which left him three points behind the Australian in the fight for the title.

Before the British Grand Prix at Brands Hatch, the Brabham No. 1 did extensive testing there and also at Snetterton and Donington Park. A spirited race resulted. Pironi and Laffite were the early leaders but Pironi stopped to change tyres whilst Laffite spun off. Jones took over and managed to hold Piquet at bay until the finish. The Australian now had 37 points to Piquet's 31 and Brands had been the first race in the second half of the Championship. As for the Constructors'; Brabham–Ford lay third behind Williams–Ford and Ligier–Ford.

Brabham took three BT49s to Hockenheim for the German *grande épreuve*, one of them being a BT49B with a different suspension set-up to the others plus the Weismann gearbox. Piquet was joined in the team by a 24-year-old Mexican, Hector Rebaque, who, after a 'rent-a-drive' season with Hesketh in 1977 had formed Team Rebaque in 1978, buying three ex-'works' Lotus 78s.

The young Mexican failed to qualify for seven of the 16 Grands Prix that year and only finished four times in the remaining nine. But at Hockenheim, in the German Grand Prix, he finished sixth – and scored a Championship point. His 1979 plans to campaign with Lotus 79s were hampered when Lotus delivered only one of the cars so Rebaque commissioned Penske Racing to design a car for him. The Rebaque HR100, Ford-powered, made its debut in the 1979 Canadian race.

Going back to 1980, the German round left the Championship wide open. Jones increased his lead by finishing third but Nelson Piquet was right on his heels in fourth place, the fourth Grand Prix in a row in which the Brazilian had scored. And Reutemann, Laffite, Arnoux and Pironi were all still in with a chance.

The Austrian Grand Prix at Zoltweg was only a week after the German race and it looked like being another battle between the favourites. Anyone believing in 'horses for courses' still had a problem: Reutemann had won in 1974 (when driving for Brabham); Jones had scored his first Grand Prix win there in 1977 in a Shadow and repeated that success in 1979 in a Williams; and Arnoux (Renault) won the pole in 1979 and was the current holder of the lap record. Murray was cheerful about the prospects. He felt the circuit suited the BT49s, but emphasised that in setting up the cars 'balance is going to be very important'.

As it happened the turbos took over, Jabouille winning for Renault and *la belle* France. Jones was second and increased his lead over Piquet to eleven points, the Brabham driver being fifth. Reutemann was third, which put him six points behind Piquet.

Rebaque had driven the BT49B in Austria, and the same car was taken to Zandvoort for him. Piquet's BT49 had a new front suspension. Both drivers had done some testing at Zandvoort prior to the Hockenheim race and Murray said: 'I think we should be quicker when we get back there.' He was right – but not before some heart-stopping moments in the Brabham pit.

In the warm-up, the mechanical fuel-pump on Piquet's car broke and the Brabham mechanics had to remove the engine (the only way to replace the pump and get it all back together again before the race started). Then they crossed their fingers. The toil and the sweat proved worth it.

Alan Jones made a second-lap error and Piquet took the chequered flag and nine points, narrowing the gap between the two of them to 2 points. Piquet's consistency could not be challenged – he had finished in nine of eleven races and scored points in all nine.

Excitement was thus nicely built-up for the Italian Grand Prix, switched that year from Monza to Imola, and there was the added bonus that Ferrari, who always made a special effort for their own Grand Prix, were toying with the idea of unveiling *their* turbo.

Brabham had a brand-new BT49 in case of any further troubles with Piquet's Zandvoort-winning car but in the event, Nelson drove the new car in the race and scored a fine victory, his second in succession, giving him a one-point advantage over Jones in the Championship. But Jones's second place (Reutemann was third) was enough to clinch the Constructors' Championship for Williams.

Brabham took four cars to Canada for Piquet and Rebaque, a race which marked the first anniversary of the former's promotion to No. 1 driver and also the first birthday of the Ford-engined BT49. There were no happy returns of the day for the Ecclestone team, however, Jones and Reutemann making a Williams 1–2 both at Notre Dame and again at Watkins Glen a week later; Piquet 'blowing up' in Montreal when he appeared to have the race in his pocket.

Perhaps justice was done anyway – because there was the matter of the nine points Jones earned but didn't get in Spain.

8

THE NAME OF THE GAME

'Piquet' is a card game for two, three or four players in which 32 cards are used. It is only the *assumed* name of the man who may well turn out to be the greatest driver of the eighties.

Nelson Souto Maior was born in Rio de Janeiro, Brazil, on 17 August 1952, to a family in comfortable circumstances. Very athletic and keen on sports, the lad showed a great aptitude for tennis and rapidly became proficient at the game. But someone introduced him to kart racing and gradually tennis receded into the background. Motor racing was now well and truly in his system but there was one major problem – his family. He knew his parents would never approve of his new interest, so he did what others have done before and will doubtless do again, he adopted a pseudonym to conceal his racing activities from his family. The name he chose was 'Piket' or 'Piquet'. It was a name he was to make famous.

He became Brasilia State 155 cc kart champion; 2-litre sports-car champion; and finally Brazilian Super Vee Champion (six victories in ten races), before coming to Europe.

After an inauspicious start – he rolled a Formula Three March at Zandvoort – he switched to Ralt (that man Tauranac again) with great success: third in the 1977 European Formula Three Championship, he became British Champion the following year with the remarkable record of eight wins, three second and two fourth places in 17 races and was runner-up for the British Vandervell Formula Three Championship, winning five races out of nine.

Piquet got his first Formula One drive in an Ensign and later in a BS Fabrications McLaren, which is when he attracted the attention of the Brabham team. He looked good enough for Bernie Ecclestone to offer him a contract as No. 2 to Lauda, and the young Brazilian was overjoyed to be associated with the great Austrian, 'I learn a lot', he beamed.

'Admiral Nelson', as some called him, did learn a lot – and he learned

There are some things a man has to do alone – like sucking lemonade through a straw.
Twice World Champion and arguably the best driver in the world: Brabham No. 1 –
Nelson Piquet.

fast. He was already outspeeding Lauda quite often, when the Austrian called it a day and walked out on the Brabham team.

The 1980 season had shown without doubt that Piquet was a Grand Prix driver of the highest class, his persistent and polished driving establishing him in the top rank. He came close to the World Championship and seemed bound to win the title one day ...

Nelson Piquet is something like the first Brabham World Champion, Sir Jack himself. He is often quiet, doesn't seek publicity, but just the same will co-operate in friendly fashion with reporters and photographers.

The Argentinian's main off-track interests are sailing, cruising and flying, and he uses his cruiser to visit his favourite holiday resort in Sardinia. He looks much younger than his age and is popular with his mechanics. How many other drivers have a fan club run by two of the mechanics? The founders of the Nelson Piquet Fan Club were Brabham 'backroom boys' Peter McKenzie and Charlie Whiting.

Just how does Piquet rate as a driver? Gordon Murray is in no doubt: 'He is the best all-round driver today – he uses his brains when he's driving.' Conceding that Nelson's pal, the little Frenchman Alain Prost, may be a little faster, Gordon still gives Nelson the edge. Since the Brabham designer's experience of working with drivers includes three other World Champions in Jack Brabham, Graham Hill and Jochen Rindt, and several 'near misses' like Carlos Reutemann, Carlos Pace and John Watson, his opinion cannot be disregarded lightly.

There is a special relationship between driver and designer. So well do Piquet and Murray work together that when there was a suggestion that Murray might be lured away from Brabham, Piquet was said to have announced that if Murray went he would go with him.

Piquet and Murray are men who attract both respect and friendship. François Hesnault, Ligier driver, respects the talent of both and states, 'They have a good sensibility, I think.'

When Michelin pulled out of Formula One at the end of the 1984 season and Brabham signed with Pirelli, Anne Routledge, of Michelin, said, 'We will miss the Brabham team – they were good to work with, Piquet, all of them. And Gordon Murray is a first-class chap.'

Piquet's first World Championship year began in Kyalami, after it had been decided *not* to take the Brabham turbo to South Africa, but to rely upon the 1980 BT49s, which had had the minimum of adjustments.

The race was run under the cloud of another FISA versus FOCA slanging-match (or was it the original fight still continuing?). The non-FOCA teams, or those whose production-car work could be jeopardised – Alfa-Romeo, Ferrari, Renault, Ligier and Osella – stayed away and the race was subsequently ruled to be of non-Championship status. It was a rough decision for the Williams team, who won the race through Carlos Reutemann.

The dispute was finally resolved in time to designate the United States Grand Prix West at Long Beach as the first round in a 15-race Championship series. The banning of sliding skirts, tighter controls on tyre dimensions, the withdrawal of Goodyear from Grand Prix racing (Michelin came to the rescue) and the increasing use of turbos meant that only a fool would put money on the outcome of the season's racing.

'It's a whole new ball game', said Murray. Brabham had three BT49Cs at Long Beach for Piquet and Rebaque, one of them with the Weismann gearbox. Piquet had been testing the cars – without skirts – at both Silverstone and Brands Hatch, but as Murray reflected: 'Nelson won here last year and we have improved the car since then. But – with the new regulations and the change in tyres we just don't know how we will be affected.'

What Murray didn't mention was that he was trying out a new hydro-pneumatic suspension and it was this that provided the biggest headache. He scrapped it after the first day's practice but this left only a day to sort things out with the old system. All in all, the team was not too disconsolate with Nelson's third place behind the 1–2 merchants, Jones and Reutemann.

Amazingly, the Williams duo did it again in Brazil, the fourth successive Championship race in which they had finished first and second. With only two races of the current season gone, they had 15 points apiece, far ahead of Piquet (scoreless in Rio) and Patrese, of the Arrows team. Meanwhile, Lotus were having trouble with their new 88, which the authorities appeared to believe offended against the new regulations. Murray, remembering how Colin Chapman had objected to the Brabham 'fan car' would have been less than human not to have a quiet smile to himself.

Nevertheless, the Brabham *equipe* felt pretty savage about Rio. Piquet started on 'slicks', was outclassed on a wet track and finished a lowly twelfth. 'We threw nine points away', he said. Points which would have been valuable later on.

The tide began to turn in the Argentine Grand Prix, although Brabham, with their own BMW turbo not yet ready, were a little concerned about some of the turbo opposition. They need not have worried – Nelson was on the bridge and in command. He stormed home the winner in Buenos Aires and repeated his victory at Imola, in a race christened with more imagination than accuracy, 'the San Marino Grand Prix'. Although from the ring Imola looked an easy win for Nelson, he revealed afterwards that he had had a lot of braking problems and to make matters worse lost his clutch half-way through. So it was a courageous victory. Another cheering note was that Rebaque brought the second Brabham into fourth place, his first Championship points since he had joined the team.

The Williams team, however, was still very much in the running, with Reutemann second in the Argentine Grand Prix and third at San Marino, whilst Jones picked up fourth place in Argentina. The Drivers' Championship table now read: Reutemann (25), Piquet (22), Jones (18). The Manufacturers' Championship: Williams (43), Brabham (25), Arrows (10).

Before the Belgian Grand Prix, the whole of the Brabham team was kept very busy. The handling problem which had emerged relative to the hydro-pneumatic suspension had to be solved, and the BMW turbo-engined car was given a try-out at Silverstone.

When Brabham got to Zolder it was to a race which turned out to be disastrous in many respects. Two mechanics were injured, one fatally. Only Reutemann of the leading drivers scored points and he won again to become the first man ever to score in 15 consecutive Grands Prix.

Monaco came next, with its long list of great competitors through the years, many of them British or Commonwealth drivers like Brabham and McLaren. Graham Hill had won the race a record five times, Jackie Stewart three, Stirling Moss three, and Brabham, McLaren, Hulme and 'Williams' once apiece. ('Williams' had no connection with the present-day Williams team or its patron. He drove Bugattis in the twenties and thirties, winning at Monaco in 1929. He was generally thought to be a Frenchman, and it was only after his death at the hands of the Nazis when he was organising French underground resistance that it became known that he was an Englishman, Captain William Grover.)

There was to be no British domination in 1981. Instead there was the surprise of French-Canadian Gilles Villeneuve winning in a Ferrari turbo on a circuit said not to be suitable for the surge of turbo power. To be fair to the pundits and without detracting from the Canadian's win, he 'inherited' the lead when a rare Piquet mistake put the Brabham into the rail, whilst Jones suffered fuel vaporisation problems in the closing stages. The Aussie hung on for second place and now the table read: Reutemann (34), Jones (24), Piquet (22).

The Spanish Grand Prix was a disappointment for Brabham, with not a point to show for it. Villeneuve won again, with Laffite (Talbot-Ligier) second and Watson (Marlboro-McLaren) third. Reutemann's three points put him further ahead in the title race.

Goodyear announced their return to Grand Prix racing before the French Grand Prix but said they would be supplying only two teams – the top two – Williams and Brabham. From the situation of one tyre manufacturer being involved there were now four.

The rain was the villain of the piece at Dijon as far as Brabham were concerned. Piquet had a useful lead when a sudden downpour caused the race to be halted. During the hold-up, the Renault team repaired Prost's fourth gear and put him on qualifying tyres. Prost is reckoned the fastest man on four wheels, and it was all he needed to sprint through the remaining 22 laps in the lead, with Piquet trailing in fifth place. Fortunately, it was decided that the two halves would count as heats and the results combined to produce the final winner. That still left Alain with the laurel wreath around his neck but placed Nelson third. The race also ended a remarkable record. For the first time since Long Beach in 1980, the Williams team failed to take a point.

Marlboro-McLaren continued their recent improvement when the scene shifted to Silverstone, John Watson scoring a popular victory. Nelson went off the track and was at first thought to have broken a leg, but X-rays revealed only bad bruising below the left knee. He also had a stiff neck. The Brabham No. 2, Rebaque, finished fifth and now had five points. Reutemann's second place put him 17 points in front of Piquet and 19 better than his team-mate, Alan Jones, the reigning World Champion.

It might be an exaggeration to say that Brabham finally got the act together at Hockenheim, but at least they had a change of fortune in the German Grand Prix, with Piquet first and Rebaque fourth. It was a fine drive by both men. Although with his usual modesty Nelson said he had been lucky because so many other people had problems, he had to overcome a lot of difficulties himself. On the opening lap, his left-hand front wing went under one of Arnoux's rear wheels, affecting the Brabham's

Nelson Piquet, in the Michelin-shod Brabham BT52B, on his way to winning the 1983 Grand Prix of Europe at Brands Hatch.

Nelson Piquet cornering during the Monaco Grand Prix of 1970. The smoothness of the modern 'slick' tyres is clearly shown – not to mention their tremendous width.

handling. Later, a piece of aluminium lying on the track tore off half the skirt on the left-hand side of the car, but Piquet, calm as ever, adapted himself to the car's pronounced understeer and came out a deserved winner. Rebaque too did well since he was without a clutch for the second half of the race.

Gordon Murray was realistic about prospects for the Austrian race: 'The Renaults should win as long as they keep going. Altitude is in their favour and the track calls for full throttle for long periods. As far as Brabham is concerned our job is to make sure of finishing ahead of Reutemann to close the gap in the Championship.' As it turned out that's more or less what happened. Laffite (Ligier) was the winner, Arnoux (Renault) second and Piquet finished third to gain two points on Reutemann, who was fifth.

The Championship position now was: Reutemann (45), Piquet (39) and Laffite (34). In the Constructors' Championship, Williams still had a massive lead of 25 points – 72 to 47 – over Brabham, but the Brabham team was in good fettle and their own turbo was nearing race-readiness – or so the manufacturers, BMW, claimed. They announced that the engine would make its debut, powering the Brabham BT50, at the Italian Grand Prix. It was reported to develop 570 brake horsepower at 10,000 rpm.

The season was building up to a terrific finish with Ligier, Renault, Brabham and Williams all going well and one or two of the others still capable of being a fly in the ointment.

Although the experts opined that sea-level Zandvoort would not suit the turbos like high-altitude Zeltweg, it was Alain Prost who won the Dutch Grand Prix in his Renault. Brabham were happy enough, however, since Piquet, by virtue of second place, joined a scoreless Reutemann in the lead for the Championship. The consistency of the Brabhams was emphasised by fourth place for Rebaque who was now eighth in the title race. Meanwhile, Rebaque was testing the new car with BMW turbo engine, but the Brabham team decided not to risk Piquet's chance of the world title by swapping horses within reach of the shore, and so it was Ford as usual for Italy. BMW were not too happy about it but common sense indicated the decision a correct one.

By a quirk of fate, Piquet's engine blew up on the last lap and he dropped from third to sixth. Lolé came third instead of Nelson and those points looked extremely valuable.

The motor-racing fraternity all crossed the Atlantic for the Canadian and Caesar's Palace Grands Prix with five drivers still in contention for the title: Reutemann, Piquet, Prost, Laffite and the reigning champion, Jones. The Brabham team were sparing no effort. Three cars were taken to Montreal, one brand new (chassis No. 15), and they had a new front-wing set-up. Some gearbox modifications had been made to try and cope with the extra demand made by the circuit on transmissions the brakes too were strengthened. Laffite won with Piquet fifth, Reutemann, Jones and Prost all failing to score. It put paid to the hopes of Jones and Prost but left the other three to fight it out on the new and untried 'car park' circuit at Las Vegas, gambling capital of the world.

The situation before the United States race was: *1*. Reutemann, Williams, (49); *2*. Piquet, Brabham, (48); *3*. Laffite, Ligier, (43).

Even victory for Jones or Prost could only give either of them 46 points, less than Reutemann and Piquet had already.

As far as the Constructors' Championship was concerned it was already the property of TAG–Williams, for there was no way that Parmalat–Brabham could make up arrears of 27 points.

In the sequel, Carlos Reutemann, the driver who had threatened to dominate the season, failed at the final test and Nelson Piquet won his first World Championship – *by a single point*. They said of him as they said of the team's founder: 'He doesn't drive faster than he has to ...'

The Williams team looked like being the stars of the show at 'the Palace', Reutemann gaining the pole with team-mate Alan Jones alongside him. But the jinx – or is it his own temperament? – which has so often hovered over the Argentinian was present again. In the warm-up he complained about the handling of his machine, although Jones was perfectly happy with his ... Lolé's car was checked over and compared with his colleague's and everything was found to be identical and in working order. But still Lolé was unhappy.

It was Alan Jones, then, who rocketed into the lead from the start – and stayed there, a Champion going out fighting. Meanwhile, Nelson Piquet soon passed the dispirited Reutemann and drew away from his rival.

In a few lines of print it all seems so simple, but in actuality the many corners of the circuit exacted a heavy physical toll from the drivers, their heads being shaken from side to side at these speeds and with these stresses. Piquet was in an awful state, being sick in his helmet several times. Certainly he was in no fit condition to withstand a challenge from Reutemann, but fortunately for the Brabham driver that challenge never came.

Whatever the reasons, Lolé finished eighth and Piquet bravely struggled on for fifth place, two points and the coveted World Championship.

9

TRIUMPH AND DISASTER

'If you can meet with triumph and disaster and treat those two impostors just the same.' So goes the saying derived from Kipling's poem; and in Nelson Piquet, the Brabham team seems to have a driver who fits the mould. Twice World Champion in five years with the team, desperately unlucky at other times, Piquet seems to take it all in his stride.

Piquet has been described by *Autocar* as having 'no superior. A couple of equals, maybe, but no one in front of him. He is very quick, very consistent, very good on all types of circuit – and as enthusiastic about his job as when he first started. That, in retrospect, is perhaps his greatest quality; he hasn't been submerged by the accruements of fame and has managed to concentrate on the things that matter to him – racing, sailing, staying quiet.'

As Peter Windsor remarked in *The Observer*: 'Niki Lauda won't admit it, but Piquet was one of the reasons he retired. He didn't need a young team-mate who lapped as quickly, if not quicker, in qualifying: Lauda wanted to be a clear No. 1 driver at Brabham, just as he had been in the early years at Ferrari. But Piquet arrived – and Lauda went.'

This is the man who has taken victory in 1981 and 1983 with pleasure but not bombast and who has accepted the subsequent disappointments of 1982 and 1984 with a smile and a shrug of the shoulders. It isn't that Piquet doesn't care, no man of his talent and professionalism could be like that, but he doesn't feel it's the end of the world and he doesn't believe that the public want him to inflict his sorrows on them.

After Piquet's Championship success in '81, the Brabham team understandably faced the 1982 season with confidence. The Mexican, Hector Rebaque, had not had a bad season with Brabham, but with an Italian main sponsor, Parmalat, it made sense to have the fiery 27-year-old Italian Riccardo Patrese as No. 2 to the new World Champion.

The cars were to be the new BT50s, equipped with the BMW turbo engines. In testing in South Africa, Piquet was said to have been timed at over 200 mph. Patrese too was impressively fast and Gordon Murray commented: 'He is probably a lot better than many people think.' But although Ecclestone and Murray now had new braces they had no intention of throwing away their old belt. Their DFV engines were still in stock and Murray said that development of Ford-engined cars would continue in parallel. The intention was to race the turbos in South Africa, go back to Ford power for Brazil and Long Beach and revert to turbos once more at Imola.

South Africa fell to turbo power as expected but they were French turbos, the Renaults of Prost and Arnoux being separated by Reutemann, now joined in the Williams set-up by Finnish ace, Keke Rosberg, who finished fifth. Lauda had emerged from retirement to join Marlboro-McLaren and he was fourth with his colleague, John Watson, sixth. The first shots had been fired in the 1982 campaign and it was Renault, Williams and McLaren issuing the challenges.

Three BT49Ds were on parade in Rio de Janeiro. The 'D' had a different monocoque from the 'C', stronger and slightly higher in front of the driver. New bodywork, aerodynamic bits and pieces and carbon fibre brakes were all part of what Murray termed 'a big winter re-vamp'. The effort was rewarded with Piquet's seventh Grand Prix victory, the Champion surviving the heat in the cockpit but fainting on the winner's rostrum. His team-mate, Patrese, was completely knocked out by the heat and retired with exhaustion.

Lauda was the winner at Long Beach with Rosberg second. Although Piquet was scoreless, Patrese was placed third after Villeneuve's disqualification. At this stage, no one was in a commanding position at the top of the table, which read: Rosberg (14), Prost (13), Lauda (12) and Piquet (9). Williams were back on top in the Constructors' battle (and had signed Derek Daly from the Theodore team to replace the enigmatic Carlos Reutemann, who had decided to retire after a long and often illustrious career) with Renault, McLaren and Brabham chasing hard.

However, not for the first time, results were being decided by committees and not by deeds on the track. Before the San Marino Grand Prix could be held, it was announced that Piquet and Rosberg were disqualified from the Brazilian Grand Prix for running under the weight limit, whilst Gilles Villeneuve was appealing against his Long Beach disqualification.

In the subsequent uproar, most of the British-based teams, claiming the rules were being changed without warning, boycotted the San Marino race and Italian spectators enjoyed a Ferrari 1-2. Even then disharmony resulted, Villeneuve claiming that Pironi passed him after both Ferrari drivers had been given the slow down and, *ipso facto*, maintain position signal.

As the circus awaited the outcome of the second most important summit meeting at Casablanca since Humphrey Bogart tipped his fedora to Ingrid Bergman, the two Brabham pilots were at Silverstone testing both turbo and Ford-powered cars. One reason was that BMW were pressing for the turbo engines to be used at Zolder.

Just about the only happy man around was the 27-year-old Chilean driver, Eliseo Salazar. The depleted Imola field meant a couple of rare points for the ATS driver, who finished fifth. Unfortunately, the team's No. 1 driver, 29-year-old German, Manfred Winkelhock, didn't share his comrade's happiness. Manfred finished sixth but was excluded from the results when his car was found to be slightly underweight.

Well, there was a race at Zolder for the Belgian Grand Prix, but just how many people were made happy by it is uncertain. It was certainly overshadowed by the withdrawal of the Ferrari team following the tragic death of their French-Canadian driver, Gilles Villeneuve, killed in a horrific accident during final practice.

The Brabham team duly heeded the voice of BMW and raced two turbos: Piquet finished fifth after losing three gears, Patrese was unplaced after losing one. The team admitted to being impressed by the reliability of the BMW engines during the race, which sounded like a piece of diplomacy as they had plenty of trouble in practice. Due to the various disqualifications, etc., the World Champion now found himself scratching around at the bottom of the table with the likes of the aforesaid Messrs Salazar and Winkelhock and a cheerful 25-year-old Brazilian rejoicing in the name of Chico Serra.

Prost, Watson, Rosberg and Lauda led the table but McLaren were appealing against Lauda's disqualification from third place at Zolder. As one entrant remarked: 'To hell with the drivers – I'm going to get me a good lawyer.'

Maybe the protagonists knew what was going on, but the general public could be forgiven for being bemused, if not bothered and bewildered.

At Monaco, Brabham aired a turbo for Piquet, a Ford for Patrese. In

Piquet at full speed in the BMW turbo-powered Brabham.

The Brabham's wheels lift off as Piquet touches the verge on a corner.

Man at work: at very high speed. This action shot brings the BMW–Brabham into fine detail.

the race, the champ had a lot of trouble, largely due to the power coming in with a bang. He eventually retired with second gear broken. Patrese, however, drove splendidly – one spin apart – and scored his first victory for Brabham, ahead of Pironi (Ferrari) and Andrea de Cesaris (Alfa-Romeo).

The seventh round was at Detroit, the first time a Grand Prix had been held in Motown. The unbelievable happened – the BMW-engined BT50, so fast in testing, failed to make the starting grid. It was a long while since any Brabham anywhere had suffered that indignity, least of all when driven by the World Champion, to boot. Patrese's Ford-engined BT49D was not disgraced in this fashion but after the race was halted, Patrese, involved in an accident following which there was a small fire in the cockpit, failed to make the re-start.

A fine drive by John Watson (McLaren) gave him the fourth Grand Prix victory of his career and European-based American Eddie Cheever brought one of the Ligiers home in second place.

The teams moved on to a Canadian Grand Prix, sadly without Canada's greatest driver. But the shadow of Villeneuve was there, the circuit on the Île de Notre-Dame being re-named in his honour, whilst Ferrari retired the number '27' in his memory. Despite the troubles in Detroit, Nelson decided to persevere with the BMW engine in Montreal against all the advice of the bar-stool experts and pen-pushing pundits. A happy decision it proved, Piquet winning from his Ford-powered team-mate Patrese, with Watson, the Detroit winner, third.

Victory was sufficient to encourage Brabhams to take three BT50s to Holland for the next round, chassis 2 and 3 plus newly-built chassis 4. The increased reliability of the BMW engine appeared to be satisfactorily demonstrated when Nelson Piquet finished second to Pironi's Ferrari.

Brabham hadn't won the British Grand Prix since 1966, when 'Black Jack' himself was the victor. That situation was not destined to be altered in 1982, both drivers being scoreless. A week later at the French Grand Prix the same dismal story repeated itself, and Brabham could only look on as McLaren, Ferrari and Renault cavorted gaily. To add to the troubles, a lot of work had to be done on Patrese's car in order to put it right for Germany after a disastrous fire at Paul Ricard, which put paid to the Italian driver's chances.

Murray & Co. had a plan which they had worked on and rehearsed and were now anxious to put into operation. In essence, the scheme was to start a race with half-full tanks (or half-empty, as a pessimist rather than an optimist would say) which, at least in theory, would give the lighter – and faster – cars a chance to establish a good lead and then, around the half-way mark, stop to refuel and change tyres. Alas, there had been little opportunity to test the theory out in recent races and it did not come at Hockenheim!

Brabham were fifth in the Constructors' Championship and their top driver of the moment, Patrese, only sixth in the Drivers' Championship.

In the Austrian Grand Prix, Piquet's engine suffered a camshaft failure and a piston came out of the side of Patrese's turbo, the car careering over the grass and stuffing itself into a bank (the grass-covered variety).

Next came the first Swiss Grand Prix in the World Championship for 28 years – since the Swiss authorities had banned motor racing following the terrible disaster at Le Mans. There had been no change of attitude – this 'Swiss' race was staged at Dijon, France, where a non-Championship 'Swiss Grand Prix' had been run in 1975 in which, incidentally, Carlos Pace had finished sixth in a Brabham.

Summing-up race prospects, one writer said: 'Neither Brabham has gone the distance in Britain, France, Germany or Austria. What price BMW turbo reliability in the hot sun of Dijon?'

What price? Both Brabhams finished this time and both finished in the points, Piquet being fourth and Patrese fifth. The engines gave no trouble but the cars handled badly and Gordon Murray and the Goodyear tyre boffins set out to solve the problem before the Italian Grand Prix at Monza. Said Gordon: 'We made a wrong choice of tyres in the Swiss Grand Prix and neither driver had enough grip.' But at last the team had been able to discover that their pit-stop scheme worked satisfactorily.

Caesar's Palace again brought the Grand Prix season to a close, but Brabham had new problems, both drivers retiring early in the Italian Grand Prix with clutch trouble. 'We've never had this problem before', sighed Murray, with the resigned air of a man expecting a bucket of paint over his head at any moment. Meanwhile, the World Championship went to the Williams No. 1 driver, Finland's Keke Rosberg.

The 1983 season opened with so many imponderables that opinions on the outcome varied from Renault's insistence that a turbo car *must* win the Championship to Tyrrell's view that a normally-aspirated Ford-powered car would do it again, just as Williams had done in 1982. Alfa-Romeo, Lotus and ATS had now joined the turbo brigade and McLaren hoped to be using a Porsche turbo later in the season, although they would start off with their Fords.

The rules had been changed – of course – the main difference being that skirts had now been banned altogether and the cars had to have flat undersides. As a result it was expected that cornering speeds, and consequently lap times, would drop. For the rest, only time could tell . . .

During the close season BMW engineers worked hard on the power plant for Brabhams, trying to reconcile the objectives of greater power with greater economy and, at the same time, improve the engine's reliability. To take the turbo, Gordon Murray had designed a narrow-bodied car with needle nose, the BT52. Piquet spent two days at Brands Hatch, testing the new car under conditions of secrecy, and then the car was unveiled at a reception in Munich, only a week or two before the first outing of the 17-race Grand Prix season, in Brazil.

Piquet had won the 1982 race and he proceeded to do so again. The Michelin-shod BT52 had a dream debut and 40,000 Brazilians cheered their local hero to victory, after he passed early race leader, World Champion Keke Rosberg, on the sixth lap.

The result left the turbo versus conventional engine argument still wide open, since Rosberg finished second and Lauda third in normally-aspirated cars.

The result also justified the practice the Brabham mechanics had had rehearsing pit-stops. When Piquet called in for new tyres and more fuel, the stop took $17\frac{1}{2}$ seconds; when Rosberg did likewise, the team almost managed to set fire to the Champion's car and only prompt work by marshals with fire extinguishers enabled him to continue. Later Keke was disqualified on the grounds that he had had to be push-started after the pit-stop.

California beckoned – and Long Beach – where Piquet had been the victor in 1980. Could he do it again? As it happened he couldn't, but it was another splendid race with John Watson charging almost from the back of the field to win, with his McLaren partner, Lauda, in second place. A sticking throttle brought disaster to Piquet who crashed into a wall when the throttle stayed on and nullified the brakes.

Ford engines had triumphed at Long Beach. The French Grand Prix at the Paul Ricard circuit was a complete reversal, turbos dominating the proceedings. Alain Prost, at the wheel of the new Renault RE40, beat Piquet by 20 seconds. Prost led the race from the start until he pitted, when Piquet took over. But when the Brabham driver made his pit-stop, Prost took over again and was never headed. The turbo triumph was complete when Eddie Cheever brought the other Renault 'works' car in third.

The San Marino Grand Prix was next, held at Imola, some 64 miles from 'the world's smallest independent republic'. Motor racing itself was the winner here because when Patrick Tambay's Ferrari crossed the line ahead of the field it was a victory enthusiastically greeted by the predominantly Italian crowd and a more than welcome shot in the arm for Ferrari. For Brabham, and especially for Patrese, who slipped up in front of his compatriots, it was one to forget.

Monaco turned out to be a struggle between four of the leading drivers of the season – Piquet, Rosberg, Prost and Tambay – after the McLarens had disappointingly failed to qualify, a rare event for them. Rosberg was the eventual winner with Piquet, Prost and Tambay following in that order, with Danny Sullivan (Tyrrell) and Mauro Baldi (Alfa-Romeo) cashing in on the absence of McLarens to take the minor placings.

For the Belgian Grand Prix, the World Championship conclave returned to the high-speed Spa-Francorchamps circuit after an absence of 13 years. Whatever the circuit, the Belgian race had never been a fortunate one for Brabham, Piquet's 1982 fifth place being their best, although Patrese had also recorded a fifth when he was with the Arrows team. The circuit had now been shortened and modernised and was less than half the length of the old Spa, but most of the drivers were enthusiastic about it.

Piquet had a rousing battle with Tambay and his Ferrari and looked good for second place until he lost fifth gear towards the end and had to settle for fourth place, Prost winning from Tambay and Cheever.

Piquet had failed to qualify for the Detroit Grand Prix in 1982; in 1983 he looked the likely winner until a few laps from the end when a flat tyre forced him into the pits and dropped him to fourth place, Michel Alboreto, of Italy, winning for Tyrrell with Rosberg (Williams) second and Watson (McLaren) third. And the Ford engines were not yet ready to abdicate in favour of turbos.

The Drivers' Championship had reached an interesting stage: Prost, with 28 points, led Piquet by just one point; Tambay was four points behind the Brazilian and Rosberg five. Watson, with 15 points, still had a chance. Renault led Williams (turbo versus normal) by four points for the Manufacturers' Championship, with Brabham, nine points behind the leaders, in fourth place.

None of the leading drivers were to win in Canada, René Arnoux scoring his first victory for the Ferrari team. Fastest qualifier, he led from start to finish, apart from a pit-stop, and his team-mate, Tambay, was third. Cheever (Renault) was second, Prost being fifth in the other Renault. Rosberg was fourth in his Williams, whilst Watson made another charge through the field to finish sixth.

Where were the Brabhams? Patrese, alas, flattered to deceive! Second for much of the race, he retired with gearbox trouble. Piquet had gone earlier with a broken throttle cable.

The British Grand Prix at Silverstone marked the half-way mark of the season and Brabham were all out to eradicate the memory of 16 years without a win in their home race. There were three new BT52Bs ready for the tussle, mid-season updates of the BT52.

'They incorporate the lessons we have learned in the first half of the season', said Gordon Murray, 'with updated suspension, bodywork and aerodynamics.' Some of the modifications had been tried out during test sessions at Silverstone and Hockenheim and on each occasion the Brabhams had been the fastest of the cars present.

At Silverstone, it was the Ferraris of Tambay and Arnoux which proved fastest in practice and started on the front of the grid. They led from the start, hotly chased by the Renault of Alain Prost. On Lap 13, Prost passed Arnoux at Copse Corner and seven laps later overtook Tambay at the same corner. Piquet was going steadily all the time and moved up into second place, temporarily taking the lead when Prost made his pit-stop. But the Frenchman, who set a new lap record of 142 mph, was not to be gainsaid and he took the chequered flag 19 seconds ahead of the Brabham No.1.

It was the first time a Frenchman had won since 1927 when Robert Benoist won the RAC Grand Prix at Brooklands in a Delage. Coincidentally, that was the year Michelin commenced production of tyres in Britain at Stoke-on-Trent – and both Prost and Piquet were Michelin-shod.

Silverstone was also the proof, if proof was needed, that on the fastest circuits normally-aspirated cars stood little chance against the turbos – five of the first six being turbo-charged.

The German Grand Prix was at Hockenheim, another fast circuit, and with Austria, Holland and Italy to follow, it looked 'curtains' for the

Two of Brabham's leading rivals in modern Grand Prix racing: the 1984 World Champion McLarens and the multi-million pound French Government-backed Renaults. In this 1983 shot, the Renault is being driven by Alain Prost, who switched to McLaren the following season.

Nose to tail: Piquet in an unusual position for him – with an adversary sitting right on his tail. But the well-balanced Brazilian is not the sort to panic. He takes it all as it comes.

Ford-powered entrants, with just a gleam of hope for the last race of the season, the European Grand Prix at Brands Hatch.

Certainly, Brabham set off for the German Grand Prix in high spirits, with Piquet's Silverstone second a recent memory and some high-speed testing on the Hockenheim circuit by Patrese, lapping in 1 minute, 50 seconds, not far outside Prost's pole time the previous year. Piquet, moreover, had set the fastest lap time in the 1982 race, going well until he tangled at the chicane with Mr Salazar, whose career is milestoned with such mishaps.

The German race did, as expected, come out in favour of the turbos but not before several of the teams running them had a great deal of trouble. The Brabham *equipe* had mixed fortunes. Piquet was in second place almost right through the race, but two laps from the end a broken fuel filter made his car catch fire and he could do little else but run off the circuit and abandon ship. Patrese had better fortune and finished third to Arnoux and de Cesaris.

Prost picked up three points, which gave him a comfortable lead in the Championship with 42 to the scoreless Piquet's 33. Tambay had 31, Arnoux 28 and Rosberg, fighting valiantly in his non-turbo car, 25.

Ferrari and Renault were now locked in battle for the Constructors' Championship, 59 points to 56, with Brabham trailing in third place at 37, one point ahead of the Williams outfit.

The Austrian Grand Prix strengthened Prost's grip on the leadership, although Piquet, with his BMW engine losing power, managed to fight off a challenge from Eddie Cheever and hang on to third place. Only half the field finished.

Most people thought Prost a certainty for the world title. He now led Piquet by 14 points whereas the Brazilian was only three points ahead of Arnoux and six clear of Tambay. There are no such things as certainties, in motor racing as in horse racing . . .

Meanwhile, Brabham had more immediate problems than the Championship race. Why had Piquet's car lost some 500 rpm during the Austrian race? Why had Patrese's car suffered from the water temperature shooting up and causing his retirement? BMW's 'detectives' were called in to work on the problems, particularly the lost revs which, apart from anything else, had resulted in Cheever nearly catching Piquet on the finishing line. Before the Dutch Grand Prix, the team went to Monza for two days testing with Piquet doing the driving.

The unbelievable happened amid the sand dunes of Zandvoort. With Piquet's engine running well he took pole position but was put out of the race when Prost braked and slid into him. Even the usually cool and calm Piquet took a while to get over that. Prost didn't gain from accidentally eliminating his nearest rival because later he was to hit the guard-rail and retire from the fray himself.

Arnoux won and moved ahead of Piquet in the title race, being just eight points behind Prost. Tambay was second and moved into a tie with Piquet. Watson's third place brought him up the table to sixth place behind Rosberg but too far behind the leaders to have Championship hopes.

There were now three races to go instead of the anticipated two – in Italy and at Brands Hatch. The South Africans had been very disappointed to lose their usual early-season date, but now, in its place, they had been rewarded with the final Grand Prix of the season on 15 October.

At Monza, the 'worked upon' Brabhams motored fast and well in practice, Patrese earning the pole position with Piquet on the fourth row of the grid. The Italian led for a long time until his engine 'blew up', when Piquet took over and stayed in front to the finish. Arnoux was second and Tambay fourth so the table now looked like this: *1*. Alain Prost, Renault, (51); *2*. René Arnoux, Ferrari, (49); *3*. Nelson Piquet, Brabham, (46); *4*. Patrick Tambay, Ferrari, (40); *5*. Keke Rosberg, Williams, (25); *6*. John Watson, McLaren, (22).

Britain's second *grande épreuve* of the year, the John Player European Grand Prix at Brands Hatch was next and Gordon Murray had a feeling that his driver wasn't yet out of the running.

'We're looking forward to Brands Hatch, it should suit us', said Gordon, 'and so should Kyalami. Nelson is in good form and only five points behind Prost so if we can provide him with reliability he can still take the title. He had a good drive at Monza, where he won, but he has driven well in so many races this season, only to be hit by problems time after time. It's easy to overlook the good drives when he has failed to finish through no fault of his own.'

As if to prove his words, Nelson put in the fastest lap of anyone, whilst testing at Brands.

The cars were little altered for the Kent circuit, apart from slight modifications to the cooling system. Piquet had BT52B/5, Patrese BT52B/6 and the spare was BT52B/1.

The outcome was that Piquet and Prost finished first and second respectively thus ensuring that the Championship would not be decided until South Africa. It was a close race early on with Patrese's Brabham narrowly leading the JPS-Renault of Elio de Angelis. However, these two were involved in an incident on the eleventh lap and Piquet went to the front. Although he had a poor pit-stop – 19 seconds – he was never seriously challenged by Prost.

It meant that three drivers still had a chance of being World Champion and all would depend upon their performances in South Africa.

Alain Prost, winner at Kyalami in 1982, had 57 points; Nelson Piquet, 1981 World Champion, 55; and René Arnoux, the outsider, 49.

As it turned out, the optimism of Murray and team manager 'Herbie' Blash was more than justified. With only two points separating them, Piquet and Prost put up a tremendous battle from the start. Nelson beat the Frenchman into the first corner and stayed in front, a record-breaking pit-stop preserving his lead. Then he was signalled from his pit that Prost had dropped out of the race so he turned his blower down, content to coast home in third place and take the title with a couple of points in hand, much safer than a death-or-glory blind dash for the chequered flag which could have foundered on an empty fuel tank. The Brabham marque won anyway, Patrese taking the flag ahead of the Alfa-Romeo of Andrea de Cesaris.

As Piquet, Murray and BMW's Paul Rosche met the Press after the race, there were comments that the Champion appeared not to have broken sweat. Thus Nelson Piquet in triumph ... Not very different from Nelson Piquet in disaster ...

Amongst the post-mortems on the season, some interesting facts emerged from the statistics published by Olivetti and Longines, the official World Championship timekeepers. They showed how well the Brabham crew had worked on pit-stops, six of the eight fastest times being down to their credit, the fastest of all being at Kyalami where Piquet was 'serviced' in 9.21 seconds. Only Lotus, with 9.62 seconds at Brands Hatch, and Ferrari, with 10.18 seconds at Zandvoort, intruded on Brabham supremacy.

Surprisingly, Tambay and Arnoux, the Ferrari drivers, and Renault's Prost had better records than Piquet in qualifying, but the Brazilian driver had the best record where it counted most – in the actual races. He was the fastest man, his race average being 99.422 per cent. The two

Brabham drivers were separated by Prost and Tambay, Patrese having an average of 98.906.

Piquet also covered the greatest distance of any driver in first position – a total of 327 laps amounting to 1,538.443 kilometres; and his Brabham partner, Patrese, covered the greatest distance in second place – 173 laps, 739.051 kilometres.

Taking the combined results of both drivers, Brabham easily covered the furthest distance in both first and second places – 409 laps in first, 334 in second.

Only when it came to reliability did the Brabhams falter. And that was true of all the turbo teams, the Ford-Cosworth teams being the most reliable.

The two Arrow drivers had the best record of finishes in relation to starts, Surer with 84.62 per cent, Boutsen with 80 per cent. Rosberg (Williams) covered the greatest distance in total – 4,006.568 kilometres, although Piquet, third, was not too far behind – 3,896.662 kilometres.

In all, the statistics seemed to prove that if Brabham could have had a turbo engine with the proven reliability of the Ford–Cosworth, the Grand Prix series could have turned into a procession.

Only one matter threatened to tarnish a magnificent year for the Ecclestone-owned team. Ferrari and Renault both protested that Brabham had used higher octane fuel than their rivals and that sometimes this had been above the legal limit of 102 RON.

FISA, backed by the French Petrol Institute, the American Society for Testing and Material and the RAC, stated that a tolerance of up to 102.9 RON was allowable and the Brabhams had never exceeded this.

Renault challenged the official conclusion, but both they and Ferrari said they were not interested in getting Brabham disqualified, only in clarification of the rules.

The general conclusion of the part of the racing world that had no vested interest one way or the other was that once again the 'on their toes' Brabham team had studied the regulations and utilised them to the best advantage, which is one of the reasons Brabham are so successful in modern Formula One racing.

10

THE SHOUTING AND THE TUMULT

Footballers often complain that their season gets longer; for motor-racing folk there is hardly a gap between one season and the next, November and December often being the only 'off duty' months. Even those months are often filled with trophy presentation, promotions of one kind or another and discussions, arguments, contract meetings and what-have-you in relation to the next term.

The close season of 1983-4 was hardly an exception. Barely had the last shot been taken of Nelson winning his second world title than frenzied activity was taking place in regard to the 1984 season.

First the Brabham team received an award, the Ferodo Trophy, which appropriately enough was received by Team Manager Mike 'Herbie' Blash and mechanic Bruce McIntosh, since it was awarded in recognition of the contribution that the slick Brabham pit-stops had made to Nelson's eventual triumph.

Such stops were to be banned for 1984, and with reduced tankage, Nelson foresaw that turbo teams would have to have computers in the pits. It would be impossible for a turbo to be raced flat-out all through a race without running out of fuel, and just as impossible for a driver to work out abstruse calculations on the amount of fuel and number of laps left, whilst at the same time trying to control and race the car. Brabham and some of the other teams had already experimented with such a system.

Most of the discussion about Brabham in 1984 centred around the question of a second driver to Nelson. Patrese was moving to join his compatriots in the Alfa-Romeo team and Ayrton Senna, the promising young Toleman driver, had been suggested as a replacement. Nelson didn't seem enthusiastic. In fact, he suggested another Brazilian, Roberto Moreno, to Bernie Ecclestone. Moreno, said Nelson, had much more world-wide experience than Senna. Piquet felt Moreno would have had a Grand Prix chance before now unless he had made the mistake of signing a three-year contract with Lotus, which kept him sidelined whilst other teams, like Williams, were looking for a driver. But Bernie didn't seem too keen on Roberto ...

John Watson was another candidate for the vacant seat. Ten years at the top and with 151 Grands Prix behind him, the Ulsterman had been fired by McLaren in favour of Alain Prost. His experience was not in question and since he had great admiration for Piquet it could be a harmonious partnership. 'A helluva talented driver,' said Watson of the Brazilian, 'a real natural. A really nice guy, he can be very amusing and has a warm rapport with his team. He just loves driving and gets on with it, without any fuss.'

But understandably, Brabham's sponsors Parmalat wanted an Italian replaced by an Italian. Whilst Watson took lonely walks by the sea at Bognor or waited by the telephone, Bernie Ecclestone would only say that Brabham's drivers would be registered with the authorities by the due date.

'Drivers come and drivers go' might have been the thought in the Brabham workshops, where two of the backroom boys, Mike Barney and Pete Bedding, had worked on the Coopers in which Jack Brabham won the world title in 1959 and 1960 and the Brabhams in which Piquet had taken the Championship in 1981 and 1983 – a remarkable record.

As the nomination day for drivers neared, the name of Teo Fabi, of Italy, was mentioned more and more as the second Brabham pilot. Fabi had driven for Toleman in 1982 and had done well on the American circuit in 1983. This, in fact, was the problem. He was under contract to an American team and some of the major races there would clash with Grand Prix dates.

Meanwhile, the Brabham BT52D made its appearance with a slightly longer fuel tank, larger radiators inside half-length sidepods and Fila sponsor labels removed. Then came nomination day and, sure enough, the name of Teo Fabi was down as Brabham's No. 2 driver. The revelation broke that he had signed a contract with Bernie Ecclestone three months earlier. He would commute across the Atlantic to fulfil his obligations there. He also had a brother who might be available to drive for Brabham should there be any conflicting clash of dates.

Teo and Corrado Fabi were both born in Milan, Teo the eldest, 29 years ago, Corrado 23. Big (the term is used in a different sense – he is a little man) brother was runner-up in the 1981 Can-Am series, made his Grand Prix debut in 1982 with the Toleman team and was runner-up in the 1983 CART PPG Championship. Corrado was 1982 European Formula Two Champion and made his Grand Prix debut in 1983 with the Osella team.

Discussions, negotiations, no South African Grand Prix at the beginning of the year ... all these things and more led to a later start to the season than usual and – technically – to a longer – five months – close season. But only if you ignore all the testing and practising which went on all over the world.

Not until 25 March, did the first race of the 1984 season – the Brazilian Grand Prix – take place. Brabham had three BT53s ready for the race and two more had already been built, so the team felt well and truly prepared. Apart from the running-gear and suspension, the car was all-new with a longer monocoque to accept the bigger fuel tank, a different turbo position and new inter-cooler system. Inevitably, there had also been changes to the aerodynamics.

Being well and truly prepared was not enough. Fabi's turbo packed up on Lap 32, Piquet's engine on Lap 34; Prost having a 40-second win over Rosberg, now turbo-charged in his Williams–Honda.

The teams moved across an ocean and 6,000 feet up for the South African Grand Prix. It was to prove another scoreless race for the World Champion and his new partner, both expiring with turbo troubles on Lap 29 and Lap 18 respectively. Piquet led for 22 laps until a pit-stop, but afterwards it was a McLaren Mardi Gras with Lauda first – his twentieth Grand Prix victory – and Prost second.

It was then back to Europe and the Belgian Grand Prix, which returned that year to the Zolder circuit. For the first time, the race provided a flicker of hope for the Brabhams. Neither car finished, but Piquet completed 66 laps and was classified tenth, whilst Fabi lasted 42 laps before he spun and could not re-start his engine.

Ferrari (Alboreto) in the once-retired 'No. 27' and Ferrari (Arnoux) were split by Derek Warwick (Renault) and for the first time in 1984 the McLarens were completely out of the picture.

Nelson Piquet posted the fastest lap in the San Marino Grand Prix but that was the only consolation Brabham could get from the race, both cars going out with engine trouble on Lap 48. Prost won for McLaren, but Arnoux in his Ferrari was close behind and the season was shaping up as a McLaren versus Ferrari contest.

Fiery Italian Riccardo Patrese, No. 2 to World Champion Nelson Piquet in the 1982 and 1983 Brabham teams.

Teo Fabi, of Italy, Brabham's No. 2 driver in 1984, made his Grand Prix debut two years previously with the Toleman team.

The French Grand Prix could so easily have been a popular French victory. Patrick Tambay earned pole position in his Renault and led until fifteen laps from the end when Lauda took over and posted McLaren's fourth win of the season. At least the trouble with the Brabham cars had been pin-pointed. It was in the turbo-waste gate area and the BMW engineers were working on it. Other BMW-powered cars were also having similar trouble, it was reported. Knowing what the trouble was and being able to do something about it were not necessarily the same thing and poor Piquet went out on Lap 11 with the old problem. For a reigning World Champion to be pointless after five rounds seemed unbelievable. This time Fabi had the consolation of being classified (ninth), still running (Lap 78) when Lauda crossed the line.

Despite everything, the Brabham team had not lost their sense of humour. After Tambay had secured pole position and the rains came down, Bernie Ecclestone went to Renault team manager, Jean Sage, and asked him to sign a petition to have another hour's qualifying session when the track dried out. Sage was wondering how to refuse diplomatically since he was quite happy with his driver on pole, when Bernie could not keep a straight face any longer and the Frenchman realised he was being had.

Monaco in June sounds like paradise even to teams which can't get their cars across the finishing line. This year Monaco was different. The rains came and would *not* go away and Clerk of the Course, Jacky Ickx, stopped the race after 31 laps. It was certainly dangerous but there were criticisms that the race had been stopped with a Frenchman in the lead who was (apparently) about to be overtaken by a Brazilian. Ickx was officially censured later.

Prost, with special Michelin 'wets', drove exceedingly well in the conditions, but Ayrton Senna, in a Michelin-shod Toleman, was closing rapidly when the proceedings were brought to an abrupt conclusion. Stefan Bellof (Tyrrell) was officially third.

Fabi 'Minor' had taken his brother's place in the Brabham team, Teo being committed in the States, but went out after nine laps with trouble in 'the electrics', perhaps not surprising with all that water around. Piquet continued for another five laps before going out with the same sort of problem.

Corrado Fabi was again in the team for Canada. He had BT53/2, the champion BT53/5 and BT53/4 was the training car. Nelson was fastest in practice but the cynics felt that was meaningless. After letting Prost get away from the line, he took the lead on the first corner. Cynics – or were they realists? – had seen that happen before. He stayed in the lead. And everyone else waited for the usual Brabham troubles to explode. They didn't happen. Nelson came home for his first win of the season, his eleventh Grand Prix victory in all.

Not until the Champion was lifted from the Brabham at the finish did everyone realise what he had endured to secure that victory. A new oil cooler had been fitted in the nose and in the confines of the cockpit the sole of Nelson's right foot was quite badly burned. Yet he had driven impeccably. Niki Lauda was moved to comment: 'Whenever I was near him he got away again. There was nothing I could do. He was quicker everywhere.'

In the euphoria of success, Paul Rosche, of BMW, revealed that the engine problems had been problems of quality control. They had been checking fuel; they had been checking the electronics; and all the time the trouble had been sub-standard spare parts.

To prove it was no flash in the pan, Piquet won again in Detroit, using the spare car, whilst Teo Fabi, back in the team, finished fourth. Nelson had dry ice jammed into the footwell to protect the right foot burned in the previous race and he nursed his car and his tyres all the way, putting on the pressure when needed, easing off when danger disappeared.

The first-ever Grand Prix at Dallas, Texas, was next on the calendar with most of the stars of the TV series on hand and, more importantly, veteran driver and designer Carroll Shelby as Race Director.

Victory went to Williams and Keke Rosberg, who combated the heat by wearing a refrigerated skull cap and sucking a tube of cold Gatorade. Piquet succumbed on Lap 45 due to a stuck throttle causing an accident, but Corrado Fabi was officially classified seventh.

Brands Hatch was next with Teo Fabi back again in place of his brother and Brabham cars which had been submitted to 'the mid-season treatment', which had proved so successful the previous year – a sort of tidying-up process. Although the modifications worked in earlier testing, Piquet had trouble getting a grip on the twisty Kent circuit and on the Friday evening the mechanics returned his car to original specification. They then had the satisfaction of seeing their driver snatch pole position from Prost.

After that the race itself was a disappointment for Brabham. Halted after 11 laps due to several crashes and cars lying on the track, the race was dominated by the McLarens following the re-start and, in the end, Lauda scored the twenty-second Grand Prix victory of his career and in doing so set a new points record of 367½. The result itself was not the most serious aspect of the matter. Piquet's engine had lost power, Fabi's put him out altogether. Gordon Murray had suffered a double disappointment. Not only had the new set-up not worked, but they had still failed after reverting to the old set-up. Such are the problems which send racing-car designers grey.

Germany was another disappointment, Piquet retiring after 23 laps (pinion bearing) and Teo Fabi after 28 (no boost pressure). Prost was first, Lauda second and McLaren were now a staggering *47 points* ahead of Ferrari for the Constructors' Championship. The Drivers' Championship also looked another certainty for McLaren, Prost and Lauda being streets ahead of their nearest competitor, de Angelis, the Lotus driver.

Time and again, Brabham had proved that they were at their most dangerous when they appeared to be on the floor, and Austria saw another example of this. True, Lauda took the chequered flag to move ahead of his team-mate, Prost, in the Drivers' table, but it was Nelson Piquet who came home second, ahead of Alboreto's Ferrari and his own team-mate, Teo Fabi. One reason for the improvement was that the trouble Piquet had had in Germany was nothing to do with the BMW turbo. 'The gearbox was all messed up,' said Murray, 'it was the first problem not related to the engine which we have had this season.' Indeed, BMW had grounds for satisfaction after the race since five of the twelve finishers were BMW-powered. In contrast, Alfa-Romeo had ten engines blow up over the weekend and Prost's TAG engine blew up in practice. It was so easy to forget that turbo power was still a comparative newcomer to the race circuit and all machinery has a period of teething troubles.

A drop in oil pressure put paid to Piquet in the Dutch Grand Prix, but Teo Fabi did well again to finish fifth. Prost won this time with Lauda second and that clinched the Constructors' World Championship for McLaren – rarely had a team taken such an inexorable grip on the title.

With three rounds to go and just 1½ points between Lauda and Prost, the only unanswered question of the season appeared to be which McLaren driver would be World Champion in succession to Nelson Piquet?

The Italian Grand Prix took heavy toll of the starting-field, 18 of the 25 dropping out, but, despite a painful back, Niki Lauda was not one of them. He took the lead six laps from the end, after engine trouble had forced out both Nelson Piquet and Patrick Tambay, and won by 24 seconds over Alboreto (Ferrari), Patrese (Alfa-Romeo) and Johansson (Toleman). Engine trouble also put paid to Teo Fabi in the other Brabham and the team looked to be heading back towards square one. Nelson kept leading races but the car did not last.

With their Championship hopes completely gone and with just two races left, Nelson, the rest of the team and Bernie were already looking forward to 1985. After all, winning the title *every other year* couldn't be bad.

Bernie Ecclestone announced that Brabham would be running next season on Pirelli tyres instead of Michelin. A couple of days later Michelin announced their withdrawal from Grand Prix racing. Behind the bald announcements were a lot of stories including the fact that McLaren, another of the teams using Michelin, had signed up with Goodyear for 1985.

Some folk opined that Michelin would have a late change of mind and agree to go on servicing the two French teams, Renault and Ligier.

As far as Brabham were concerned, they had tried out Pirellis during testing sessions at the Nürburgring as well as the Michelins they would use for the last two Grands Prix of the 1984 season. Nelson Piquet achieved fourth fastest time of those present with a lap of 1 minute, 20.46 seconds, and it transpired that this time had not been done on Michelins but on Pirelli 'qualifiers.'

Announcing that Brabham and Pirelli had signed a three-year contract, Bernie Ecclestone commented: 'We have followed the progress of Pirelli during the 1983 and 1984 seasons and feel sure that their association with a competitive team will lead to the same results as they have achieved in all the other categories they have been associated with.' The contract was said to be an extremely lucrative one – for Brabham.

Important although tyres are, Gordon Murray was still thinking of that elusive reliability – 'we've led the last five Grands Prix but we haven't won any of them.'

So it was back to the Nürburgring for real, this time the European Grand Prix on a circuit much altered from the old formidable 'Ring. Most of the teams and drivers had to take a back seat in the struggle between Lauda and his team-mate, Prost, for the World Championship, 63 points for the Austrian against the Frenchman's $52\frac{1}{2}$. Even that battle took second place to the media's somewhat grisly preoccupation with the fact that Lauda would be driving at the Ring for the first time since that terrible 'flamer', which had threatened his life and left him badly scarred. Lauda himself bore the never-ceasing interviews and questions with great good grace, shrugging his shoulders with the words, 'I am a professional.'

There was one heart-stopping moment in the race when Lauda spun but he recovered and went on his way. Prost was the winner which meant that it would all be on the last race in Portugal to decide which of the McLaren drivers would succeed Nelson Piquet as World Champion.

Prost led pole-winner Piquet off the line and was never headed. Lauda trying to overtake back-marker Mauro Baldi (Spirit) spun in clouds of smoke. 'Baldi chopped me', he said. 'He didn't see me coming and moved over. I had no alternative but to spin.' As the Renaults of Tambay and Warwick faltered, Lauda moved up into fourth place and he was so very very near to being second since Alboreto and Piquet ran out of petrol but, fortunately for them, just a few yards beyond the finishing-line. With smiles on their faces, the Italian and the Brazilian got out of their stranded cars, expressively shrugged their shoulders and embraced. It was yet another illustration that despite all the money involved in modern sport, participants still have sporting instincts.

It was also an illustration that so highly complicated is the modern racing car, not to mention the regulations, that the belief of Piquet and others that pit-men will have to use computers in future to calculate the mixture of turbo power and fuel required to get a car to the finish is not far-fetched.

Prost and Lauda must have looked forward to Estoril with mixed feelings if only because Piquet, Alboreto and others out of the running were still good enough and fast enough to make it awkward for the McLaren duo in the culminating *grande épreuve* of the season.

The final shoot-out at the old Estoril corral attracted more media attention than ever and with a fortnight's gap between the European Grand Prix at the Nürburgring and the Portuguese race, newspapers and magazine were crammed with interviews and articles featuring the two main protagonists, Lauda and his team-mate, Prost.

Following FISA's decision to allocate points won by the disqualified

Tyrrell team to the next drivers in line – a decision which gained another point for Prost – the leading positions in the Driver's Championship prior to Estoril were as follows: *1*. Lauda, McLaren–TAG, (66); *2*. Prost, McLaren–TAG, (62½); *3*. de Angelis, Lotus–Renault, (32); *4*. Piquet, Brabham–BMW, (28); *5*. Alboreto, Ferrari, (27½); *6*. Arnoux, Ferrari, (27).

It meant that if Prost won, Lauda would have to finish second to take the Championship. If Lauda did not finish in the first six, Prost would still have to be at least third to take the title. The odds looked to be on the Austrian – but motor racing is a funny game. Said team boss Ron Dennis, 'It all comes down, to fate.'

The Constructors' Championship was already settled. No matter what Ferrari, Lotus and Brabham did in Portugal, no one could catch McLaren who were already *74 points* ahead of their nearest challenger.

To the Brabham team there was one consolation in the limelight being focused on McLaren – they were able to get on with their work untroubled by the TV cameras, the instant experts and all the rest of the media circus. And, for those who believed in omens, the last time a Grand Prix had been held in Portugal (1960) it had been won by the founder of the team, 'Black Jack' himself.

Until the race was over, Nelson Piquet was still the reigning World Champion, as fast as Prost, as wily as Lauda, as good as or better than both in the eyes of many. Given the reliability of the TAG turbos, few doubted that Piquet would still be in the running.

Meanwhile, there was the challenge of fighting for the pole. Eight times Nelson had gained the pole during the year and he badly wanted to make it nine. There were problems ... mostly with the rain. As the clouds came up, Nelson yelled for qualifying tyres, 'Queek, queek'. But 'queek' though the Brabham mechanics were, the rain was 'queeker'. Nelson kept one eye on the weather. When a glimmer of sun appeared, he changed from 'wets' to 'slicks' and did a few gentle warm-up laps. As soon as the track dried out he was off, posting a fast time. He would have put up a faster one still had he not gone into a hairpin curve and found a Renault slewed across the track. Such things are all in the day's work for the Brazilian and eventually he posted the fastest time of them all, 1 minute, 21.703 seconds, to secure pole position for the ninth Grand Prix of 1984. Prost was 0.071 seconds behind him and 0.162 seconds ahead of Brazil's other star driver, Ayrton Senna (Toleman).

With Brabham's No. 2 driver, Teo Fabi, jetting back to Italy because of his father's death, the team were lucky to secure the services of an adequate replacement in the second car.

Stefan Bellof was the first name considered but he could not be tracked down. What about Manfred Winkelhock? He had left the ATS team and although he was rumoured to be heading for the RAM outfit, he didn't have a ride for the Portuguese race. Manfred was at home in Germany, the telephone handy, and, yes, he could come.

But Stuttgart was fog-bound and he could obtain neither a light aircraft to charter nor a commercial flight. So he hired a car and drove to Estoril, arriving late on Friday night and learning the course – in the dark – on the hired car. After all that, he did well to qualify nineteenth fastest.

For Lauda, qualifying could have been a disaster which cost him the championship. After sitting in the pits for a long while as electricians dealt with a faulty switch, Lauda, under pressure, could not come up with a really fast time.

Prost was on the front row with Piquet, Lauda (qualifying eleventh) was on the sixth row. It meant the Austrian would have to work his way through the field to catch Prost but then he is a past master at that.

A delightful story was circulating that Prost, at the end of Saturday's practice, had suggested to Nelson Piquet that it would be helpful if they avoided a starting-line shunt in their efforts to be first away. Nelson gave his innocent boyish smile and delivered the riposte, 'Sure, no problem, you just let me go first.'

Funnily enough, in the event neither of the front pair made a good start. Prost, with one eye on Piquet, missed a gear. Piquet, with one eye on Prost, made a slow start – and it was former champion, Keke Rosberg, of Finland, who blasted past both of them into the lead. In another moment of aberration, rare for the Brabham No. 1, Nelson spun off before the end of the first lap and was left at the tail-end of the field, although fortunately he was able to re-start.

Prost, however, had recovered himself and after eight laps went past Rosberg into the lead. Mansell took up the chase in his JPS Lotus-Renault and the British driver looked an odds-on-favourite for second place, although unlikely to catch Prost who was going like an express train. Behind them two men were carving their way through the field. One was Lauda and he was the one Prost had to worry about. The

Piquet, all ready to go, at tyre trials at Brands Hatch during the 1984 season. Such
trials are a regular feature of the Grand Prix circuit today.

The view of a Brabham which is the one most of the Grand Prix drivers see these days.
Sponsors Parmalat make sure their message reaches the public.

Austrian lay in wait for driver after driver, lurking on their exhaust pipes, probing their defences and then in a swoosh of power, sweeping past them.

Johansson (Toleman), Alboreto (Ferrari), Rosberg (Williams) and Senna (Toleman) – all succumbed to the same darting attack. Finally, only Mansell remained between Lauda and Prost, but as long as the Englishman occupied second place, Lauda could not be champion. Then, with 52 laps gone, Mansell's cruel luck struck again as his brakes went. The Lotus pulled into the pits and Lauda was where he wanted to be – in second place. He was content to stay there. If Prost kept going and won, Lauda would be champion by finishing second. If Prost dropped out, Lauda had only to finish to be Champion.

The two red-and-white cars circulated steadily until the flag with the Frenchman the winner and the Austrian the Champion by the slenderest margin ever – one half of one point. 'If the difference had been more, it would have been unfair', said McLaren designer John Barnard.

It was tough luck on Prost, defeated for the second year at the last hurdle, a driver whose Portuguese win enabled him to equal the record of Jim Clark in winning seven Grands Prix in a season and who had the hopes of France riding on his shoulders as he strove to become his country's first World Champion.

The second man working his way through the field, forgotten as attention focused on Lauda, was Nelson Piquet. From last in the race he worked his way up to sixth and a Championship point, an achievement lost in the McLaren celebrations but one which underlined Piquet's ability and the prospects that Brabham might again have a World Champion in 1985. For once, both cars lasted the race, Winkelhock driving steadily to finish tenth.

Nelson's solitary point was in some respects a gift from Renault who added the finishing touches to yet another unhappy race for them by failing to signal Patrick Tambay, then in sixth place, that Piquet was gaining on him. Tambay was under the delusion that he was sure of sixth place and that if he made sure of finishing one or two of the others ahead of him might drop out, enabling him to do even better. Whilst he was thus musing, Piquet swept past . . .

Manfred Winkelhock was delighted with his tenth place. 'I did more laps in practice than in my last three races for ATS. Then to finish the race itself . . .'

For Teo Fabi, it meant more than the death of his father. He had previously said that he would race three more years before taking over the family business. Furthermore, he had decided to give up racing in the States in order to concentrate on his drive with Brabham on the Grand Prix circuit. Now those plans might have to be shelved . . .

11

BERNIE

He is a tough-talking, jet-travelling, middle-aged whizz-kid, a diminutive figure in large horn-rimmed spectacles. His name is Bernard Ecclestone and he is the most powerful man in Grand Prix motor racing today.

Ecclestone is the owner of the Brabham team, one of the most successful in Grand Prix racing. That would be enough for many men. But Bernard Ecclestone's real power arises from being the top man of the Formula One Constructors' Association. Unless Bernard Ecclestone says 'Yes' no one – but no one – runs a Grand Prix anywhere in the world. Correction, they may run a race, but most of the world's best drivers and most of the world's best cars won't be there unless the Ecclestone seal of approval is clearly marked on the packet.

Bernard Ecclestone hates personal publicity. His private life is his private life and 'of no interest to anyone else' (which may not be strictly true). There may not physically be much of Ecclestone, but he looms large over other adminstrators in the sport in terms of public interest and speculation. So, ironically enough, does his oft-time opponent and adversary, Jean-Marie Balestre, President of the FISA, official controlling body of the sport. Of which, more anon ...

Bernie Ecclestone, as a youngster, was a keen motor cyclist and, like many others, before and since, tried his hand at racing. The necessity to earn a living led him to combine pleasure with work and he opened a motor-cycle dealership in South London. Post-war motor racing was getting under way, as mentioned earlier, with the 500 cc or 'Half-Litre' brand of competition in which the Coopers, father and son, were prominent. As, basically, cars with motor-cycle engines were used, it was not surprising that some of the people involved had more of a two-wheel background than four. Bernie Ecclestone was one of them. Harold Daniell, the TT rider, was another.

Bernie may not have been the world's greatest driver but, as in everything he did, he applied himself to the task in hand. On 23 June 1951, he was second to John Cooper in a heat of the Brands Hatch Open Challenge race and defeated Grand Prix driver-to-be, Stuart Lewis-Evans in a heat of the *Daily Telegraph* Trophy. He and Stuart were close friends which, eventually, led to a 'what-might-have-been' story . . .

Dean Delamont remembers the young Mr Ecclestone from those days. 'He didn't hang around much. He came, raced and then went back to South London to sell motor cycles.'

John Cooper is another who remembers Bernie well from those days. 'Funnily enough, I knew Bernie Ecclestone long before I knew Jack Brabham. Bernie bought a 500 cc Cooper from us, then another and then a Cooper–Bristol, if memory serves me correctly. I used to think he was a flash gent because he had all the gear and was always painting and chrome-plating his cars. On one I seem to remember he chromium-plated the wishbones which I though was a dangerous practice because of the risk of crystallising.

'But he tackled his racing in the way that he tackles everything else – with great attention to detail and with all his concentration. And at the end of the day's racing off he would toddle to resume selling motor bikes at his South London dealership.

'He and Roy Salvadori were great chums and were the great gamblers of the time. Any vacant moments – and out would come the cards.

'Bernie was – and is – a shrewd business man and went on from motor cycles to cars and later to property, I believe. Roy Salvadori at one time had a car showroom selling Aston Martin and fancy machinery like that and Bernie would walk in and say, "That one – and this one – and that one over there. I'll give you four grand for the lot."

'But if you asked me the most striking thing about Bernie, I think I would have to say that he has a brilliant brain.'

But the racing bug had bitten fairly deeply that summer. A week later, Master Ecclestone was at Boreham, subsequently to become the Ford test-track, where, at a West Essex Car Club meeting, he was second in his heat and third in the final to Eric Brandon and Alan Brown, two of the top dogs at the time. On 6 August, back at Brands, Bernie won his heat of the Open Challenge, but rain intervened and the meeting was abandoned before he had a chance to show what he could do in the final.

Bernie Ecclestone bobbed up again at the Brighton Speed Trials with a worthy second in the 500 cc class, and at Brands on 9 September was second to Ken Carter in the final of the Open Challenge. Don Gray was third and Lewis-Evans fourth. That was pretty much the highlight of the Ecclestone racing career but little could dampen his enthusiasm for the sport.

However, it was to be 1958 before he again figured on the motor-racing scene with any degree of prominence. Connaught, backed by a member of the McAlpine building family, had been trying hard to put Great Britain on the Grand Prix map, and Tony Brooks had driven one of the cars to victory in the Syracuse Grand Prix of 1955. Although it was not a World Championship event, it was the first win by a British driver *in a British car* in a genuine Formula One race since Segrave won the Spanish Grand Prix in a Sunbeam in 1924. 'Williams' (William Grover) and Dick Seaman had scored Grand Prix wins in the intervening years but at the wheel of French and German cars respectively.

Rodney Clarke, the design-genius behind the team, lacked adequate finance and when the limited McAlpine support was withdrawn the Connaught team was in serious difficulties. John Webb, present-day Brands Hatch supremo, started a fund to save Connaught but it was in vain, works and cars were sold and Connaughts vanished for ever from the Grand Prix scene.

The man who bought the cars was Bernie Ecclestone, whose business interest were flourishing. A move little publicised at the time – the sale might have ensured the continuance of Connaught. Bernie intended to race the cars and his friend, Stuart Lewis-Evans, who had commenced his Grand Prix career with Connaught before moving to the ever-improving Vanwall team, was to be the No. 1 driver.

Alas, Lewis-Evans died from injuries received after his Vanwall crashed in the Moroccan Grand Prix and Ecclestone, showing a soft core which none of his critics ever believe is there, dropped the project! 'Stuart, my good friend, had been killed and that ended my interest.'

It was not a passing phase. Something like 14 years were to elapse before that interest would be revived to the extent that the South London entrepreneur would reappear on the Grand Prix scene as a car owner; and that would be when he bought Motor Racing Developments and the Brabham team from Ron Tauranac.

Brabhams were in a trough at the time and it is doubtful if anyone around the circuits was greatly concerned, one way or the other, about the 'newcomer'. They were in for some shocks.

After a tentative season or two, Bernie had the Brabham team in good shape and it has remained through more than a decade one of the most consistently successful teams of them all. But Ecclestone stood back, took a look at the sport as a whole and wasn't satisfied with what he saw. To a man who had developed profitable motor-cycle, car and property companies, motor racing was in a mess.

The root of it all was that the sport, like so many other sports, was controlled by amateurs, many of them elderly, some from countries which had little or no motor sport. Between the wars, Brooklands had been run on the slogan of 'The right crowd and no crowding'. Many of the sport's rulers, especially on the Continent, still had that attitude.

Dean Delamont who, in his days as the RAC's chief motor-sport executive and delegate to international committees and conferences, had to exercise great diplomacy, pulls no punches in retirement. He believes that there are still too many amateurs in positions of authority, even after the reorganisation which has taken place.

'The real problem, as I see it, is that FISA don't know enough about the sport to control it adequately. Basically speaking, you've still got the same idea as you have in many sports where the government of that sport comprises a lot of amateur gentlemen who really go to the meetings because it gives them a chance to travel.

'I believe this sort of attitude is at the root of matters like the Tyrrell affair [the Tyrrell team were suspended after alleged offences involving fuel and weight].

'Tyrrell were probably doing what all teams do – studying the regulations including all the fine print (and there's lots of that) and then constructing their cars and setting them up so as to get maximum performance within those regulations – but going to the limit with no leeway. But the regulations are now so complicated that there are arguments over interpretation. And I'm afraid that too many people at the FIA and FISA don't know much about motor racing and don't understand their own regulations.'

If that is the situation today, it most certainly was the situation in the early seventies and there were genuine fears that Grand Prix racing might easily go to the wall. Manufacturers and drivers were asking for more money, national auto clubs and circuit-owners were saying that no money was available.

The Formula One Constructors' Association, with Bernie at the helm, sorted that one out, although not without the most tremendous struggle.

'There were so many people in the game living in the past and talking about good old "amateur" sport and tradition and good taste. Those days have gone. There are no amateur sports today. Why, the biggest money-making business of them all is the "amateur" Olympic Games', raps Ecclestone.

'When we started to commercialise motor racing, these critics and traditionalists complained about sponsorship and TV coverage and high admission charges, they complained about advertising on the cars, the drivers' overalls and the circuits. They complained about every commercial aspect of Grand Prix promotion.

'Well, of course we could wear our hats the wrong way round and drive in shirt-sleeves and have no advertising but that would mean that only those with enough money to own race cars would be able to race.'

With this philosophy, Bernie Ecclestone sold his fellow-constructors, or most of them, on the idea that it was better for them to deal with the circuit-owners as a body, a trade union if you like, of racing-car manufacturers. Until then, it was usual for individual teams to conduct their own negotiations for starting-money, most of the prize money being modest. Promoters who had secured the services of the top contenders would drive a very hard bargain with the more lowly teams, needed to complete a full field.

By joining together and negotiating as FOCA, the constructors were in a much stronger position to obtain good terms. Nor was the traffic all one way. The promoter needed to deal with only one person – Bernie – and that one person could deliver a package of virtually a complete field.

Thus, through the seventies, both starting-money and prize-money increased dramatically. The next logical step came around 1978 when FOCA, in effect, became promoters themselves and responsible for the entire operation of some of the Grands Prix. It worked well and the number of races for which FOCA delivers a complete package has steadily increased.

Not that it has been as simple as it sounds. There have been clashes with the Grand Prix Drivers' Association, now won over and moribund, and with 'Iron Man' Balestre and the FISA.

Even that relationship is much happier today. Says Bernie, 'They are not as old as they were and more motivated. The last two or three years have been quite good. We have this agreement with FISA known as 'Concord' and it has given the sport more stability than in the past.

There is also the Formula One Commission on which everyone involved is represented and can make their views known.'

The sums of money involved today all have noughts on the end, lots of them. Just how much everything has gone up in real terms is· difficult to assess. Dean Delamont again: 'Probably if you relate the money in motor racing today to inflation it is not all that much more. If you think of the values of 1954 compared to 1984, I don't know how many scores of times things have gone up. There's more money in the teams in general because there's more interest in them, but if you actually look at the cost of sponsorship I think when Coopers first won the World Championship they had a seasonal budget of about £50,000.'

Bernie Ecclestone estimates that today it costs an English-based team, ten to twelve *million* dollars per season. And the days have long gone when you could get five, or even three, dollars to the pound. 'Renault and Ferrari spend more than double that amount', claims Bernie.

Although prize-money has increased dramatically, most of the money comes from sponsors – cigarette companies, dairy firms, brewers – with support also from tyre and accessory manufacturers; and from television.

What do the sponsors get out of it? In the case of the cigarette manufacturers motor-racing sponsorship provides a shop-window denied them by the ban on TV advertising. For other sponsors it means TV exposure, mobile billboards circulating in front of hundreds of thousands of people and a bridgehead towards a 'with it' section of the community with tremendous purchasing power.

Those sponsors who are in the motor industry themselves, the tyre and accessory manufacturers, make advertising capital when their team scores a victory or wins a championship. Carbon fibre, for instance, has come to be used more and more in Formula One construction. It is easily moulded and formed, reduces weight and, it is claimed, increases strength. So when Nelson Piquet won the World Title for the second time, Courtaulds were quick to announce that their Hysol Grafil carbon fibre had been used in the winning Brabham. They announced, '[We] are proud to have been associated with the development and design of the extremely successful Parmalat-Brabham BT52B.'

This type of supporter of motor racing is looking for more than advertising value from participation. Michelin, on whose tyres Brabham were running in 1984, said when they announced their retirement (temporarily, one assumes) from the Formula One scene: 'Michelin's objective in Formula One was to test the versatility of its radial technology and this has been fully achieved. Since the company's debut in 1977 there have been 59 victories and four World Championship titles won on Michelin radial tyres.'

Said spokeswoman Anne Routledge: 'Winning on Michelin brings prestige for both the competitor and the tyre company. The tyre performance is closely monitored throughout practice and racing, precise notes being made concerning tyre pressures, temperatures and wear rates. In addition the state of the vehicle is closely followed, the performance recorded, the nature of the road surface examined and, finally, the driver's comments noted. All this information is collated and it allows the research department to check the tyre's progress and ensure that the overall development programme moves forward.'

Castrol, the oil company, has a similar outlook in that sponsorship brings publicity, aids development and, ultimately, increases sales. Says spokesman Derek Guy: 'Castrol sponsored Brabham in 1983 and 1984, the contract covering advertising rights in respect of the team and drivers and we do, of course, have Castrol identification on the cars.

'Behind this is the fact that Castrol is the only lubricant approved by BMW for their Formula One and Formula Two engines. The product which we use is B353 which is an SAE 40 lubricant blended from castor, synthetic and mineral products. There is a long history connected with the blend so that you can see that the sticker on the car is only the tip of the iceberg.'

Bernie and FOCA keep a close watch on television and are constantly seeking ways and means of improving the quality of the coverage. At Estoril in 1984, the latest of many ideas in filming from the cars themselves, was tried out. Winkelhock's Brabham was fitted with a 3.5 kg British-built video camera, mounted just above the driver's right shoulder and smaller than previous units. A transmitter beamed the signal to a helicopter acting as a satellite above the track. Winkelhock drove the Brabham in a special 20-minute session and picture quality was described as 'unbelievably good'. David Earl, the man behind the project, envisages making the camera so small that it can be fitted to, say, downhill skiers.

It is a measure of Ecclestone's success in converting motor-sport interest and enthusiasm into TV coverage and hard cash that so many major sponsors have jumped on the Grand Prix bandwagon. Without them Grand Prix racing would be an impossibility today. This could readily be seen when Tyrrell's monthly budget figures were disclosed during the 1984 season:

	£
Engine rebuilds	30,615
Gearboxes and spares	7,469
Production materials	19,082
Sub-contracting	9,210
Wages and salaries (including directors)	45,456
Company pensions	1,539
Director's pensions	35
Health plans	630
Employer's insurance	278
Freight and insurance	6,742
Travel and accommodation	12,842
Development and testing	12,070
Capital expenditure for vehicles	0
Capital expenditure on plant	3,500
Road tax, licences and insurance	262
Vehicle repairs, petrol	2,234
Plant repairs and renewals	1,768
Sponsors' expenses	3,102
Bank charges	66
Insurance for factory	103
Rates, electricity and heating	1,167
Repairs to premises	478
Postage	492
Telephone and telex	992
Legal fees	300
Audits	221
Miscellaneous	221
Team uniforms	192
total	161,114

A monthly expenditure of that order comes to nearly £2 million for the year. Bear in mind that this is one of the most economically-run teams in the business (Tyrrell have a work-force of about 45, roughly half the number at Williams and McLaren and a quarter of those employed on the Grand Prix teams of Renault and Ferrari); that the figures do not include the drivers' retainers; and that Tyrrell in 1984 was the only team running on the normally-aspirated Ford–Cosworth engines and they had no new engines to buy (in 1983 they had spent £340,000 on them). It can easily be seen that for the bigger teams Bernie Ecclestone's estimate of ten to twelve million dollars for a season is no wild claim. Bernie won't give a detailed breakdown of his or anyone else's expenditure, 'I know how I run my team. I don't know what others do.'

Not that he is entirely disinterested in other people's money. As Chief Executive of FOCA he is on a percentage of what money that organisation brings in, some say 2 per cent. That doesn't initially sound a lot – but work it out.

It certainly enables Bernie, who cannot have been short of a pound or two (before FOCA), to live the life of a jet-propelled tycoon, with, literally, the latest in jet aircraft at his disposal.

Bernie Ecclestone had a mansion in Kent but said he was going to get rid of it – he didn't get any time to get down – and he has a fabulous penthouse almost opposite the House of Commons. His living-room has a two-storey high ceiling with a gallery at the back leading to the bedrooms. One wall is covered by a specially-commissioned copper sculpture or bas-relief, for, perhaps surprisingly for a man so engrossed in motor sport, he is also greatly interested in art of all kinds. Those who have been his guests at the penthouse come away impressed with the apartment and even more with Mrs Ecclestone, a charming hostess and producer of fabulous meals. She isn't seen too much around the motor-racing circuits, although she told a mutual friend she much enjoyed Monaco.

It would be a mistake to imagine that Bernie Ecclestone, top man of FOCA, is so tied-up with international affairs that he leaves the running of the Brabham team to others. Far from it. It is *his* team. And *he* is the boss. He has confidence in his designer, his team manager and his work-force. But he still wants to know everything that is going on and he is still the man who makes the major decisions ... sometimes the minor ones too.

Bernie regards the constant detailed alterations which designer Murray makes to the Brabham cars as having two purposes: one, obviously, to make the cars go faster and last longer; the second, to increase public interest. 'A lot of the motor-racing public are keen on technology. Every race hundreds of things alter and this creates interest. It gives the Press something to write about and gets people talking about Grand Prix racing and actually going to the events.'

Engines have been a bigger problem to the Brabham team in recent years rather than chassis. 'We had a lot of trouble with the Alfas – my goodness, yes. We had a lot of trouble with the BMW engines and we are still having problems with them now. The Porsche and the Ferrari are the most interesting turbos because they have been designed for car racing. BMW and others use a standard block, and the configuration obviously restricts what you can do with it.' As this is written, Ecclestone's notable lack of enthusiasm for some of the turbos may yet lead to a return to normal aspiration with Ford.

Bernie's evaluation of Brabham drivers may surprise some people . . .

'The best? It's very difficult to say . . . but . . . Nelson.

'The most underrated, without a doubt, was Hector Rebaque. He would fly over from Mexico just before practice – and the time-lag is ten hours or something like that – and do wonderfully well. He just wasn't serious enough about it. He didn't care if he raced or not. That's why we parted company. The ability was there but he wasn't serious about it.

'Reutemann was very good, of course, but a victim of his own temperament.

'Lauda was all right. Yes, he did walk out on us in Montreal, but he was very easy to get along with and highly intelligent. One of the best.

'Carlos Pace, who was killed in an air accident, was super. He was with us at a very difficult time and did wonderfully well under the circumstances. Then, just as things were getting better, he was killed.

'It is not true that we have had a lot of "rent-a-drive" fellows. We don't believe in it. At the same time we do heed the wishes of our sponsors. If your main sponsor is Italian (as ours is – Parmalat) then it is only natural that they would like to see a fellow-countryman driving at least one of the cars. That's why we had Teo Fabi this year, for example.'

Dean Delamont thinks Bernie Ecclestone's attitudes are reflected in the Brabham team: 'I've always regarded Bernie as a perfectionist. If you look at the cars today they are so far away from the John Cooper–Jack Brabham era. At one time, from the engineering standpoint, I always thought that Ferrari were the masterpieces, but if you look at the present-day Ferrari it is made more like the old Cooper with bits-and-pieces welded together.

'Mind you, Colin Chapman was the exponent of making welded bits

- there's nothing really wrong with making welded structures as long as they are properly designed. But there's so much machining and meticulous engineering in the current Brabham that it is probably the most elaborately manufactured car on the starting-grid. I think this is typical of Bernie because in everything I've seen him do he's been a perfectionist.

'Not only the cars but his attitude both to racing and to business where he believes in winning ... yes, he likes winning, obviously, and he likes playing cards and winning. He and Teddy Mayer (former McLaren chief now associated with Roger Penske Racing) were the noted card-players on all the airline trips.'

Not everything Ecclestone has done in motor racing is purely money-orientated. He has been - and is - concerned with the sport's image, value given to the public and the safety of the drivers.

A consultation with a leading neurologist, Sid Watkins, who is also a motor-racing enthusiast, led to the latter's appointment as Medical Consultant to FOCA. Now, not a Grand Prix race anywhere in the world can start until Sid has personally approved all the medical services and facilities.

How does Bernie see the future?

'As long as politics are not allowed to kill common sense the sport is certain to expand. We could be at the launch of a new era.

'We're just getting Formula 3000 off the ground [a formula which will provide a training-ground for up-and-coming potential Grand Prix drivers and a use for old Formula One engines], but it has taken *two years* to get the idea past a lot of incredibly stupid people.

'The main trouble is that each is looking after itself instead of looking at matters overall. If the overall picture is right then we shall all be all right individually, Alas, some of them can't see that! They look just for the short-term results. Of course, some are owned by companies and you can understand the pressures on them.'

All the time, Bernie seeks to advance the cause of motor racing internationally. He has had discussions with Hungary and with the USSR and - as this was written - he was sitting at a table with South Australian representatives, in Britain to discuss terms for an Australian Grand Prix. Such is his reputation that even a bunch of tough Aussies had viewed their coming meeting with some trepidation.

There is a feeling that Bernie has deliberately cultivated the myth of his ruthlessness, his irascibility and his hardness and that, underneath, is a kindly, warm-hearted man. But the myth gives him a couple of points lead in the bargaining stakes.

Bernie Ecclestone and Teddy Mayer have been jokingly referred to as the 'Mafia of motor racing'. Joke or not, Dean Delamont strongly disagrees. 'I would not have thought that was an accurate description. I've always thought that he was an honest man. Certainly I've always had straight dealings with him and reasonably straight talking. I think he is an extraordinary man. He has the most fabulous memory for details and he never seems to tire. Whether in the five years since I've had much to do with him the physical strain has got to him I don't know. In those days he never tired.

'I hope and believe that the work he has done in bringing FOCA and FISA together will endure. I think they need each other in the way that the TUC really needs the CBI. I hope they'll work together more amicably than those two organisations do, but from the standpoint of the race organisers, FOCA's a jolly good idea. It gives the race organiser the opportunity of getting a proper package, it has helped in sponsorship negotiations, it has helped in television coverage and I think it has helped generally towards the popularity of the sport.'

12

EPILOGUE

by John Cooper
President of the British Racing and Sports Car Club

Motor racing has changed out of all recognition in the period of this book and the lifetime of the Brabham racing team. To compare the cars of the fifties with those of the seventies or the drivers of the fifties with those of the seventies is an impossible task – it's a completely different ball game.

Jack Brabham and his little New Zealand pal, Bruce McLaren, will always be special to me. Bruce, alas, has gone but Jack is still with us, a great guy as well as a great driver.

Leaving them aside I still think I would have to name Fangio as the greatest of them all, although Jim Clark and Jackie Stewart were pretty good. Jochen Rindt was, I think, the fastest of them, although Ronnie Peterson too was very quick.

The driver today who most reminds me of Jack is the 1984 World Champion, Niki Lauda. Jack could be relied upon to do his best to win without doing anything silly and I see a lot of him in Lauda.

If positions had been reversed in the final Grand Prix of 1984 and Prost had been third to Lauda and Mansell, needing to be second to take the title, I could envisage the Frenchman going flat out to pass Mansell – and probably running out of fuel.

Lauda handled it as I imagine Jack would have done, coolly and logically. He said to himself: 'Mansell's only finished a couple of races this season, why should this race be any different? I'll just sit here and wait for the bugger to blow up.' Which, in effect, was what happened.

Some aspects of the game today I find disturbing if not frightening. I'm not too impressed with the way things are handled. Without raking over the ashes of the Tyrrell affair I feel it could have been better handled.

The cost of Grand Prix racing is astronomic today. Cooper first won the World Championship on an annual budget of £50,000, today some of the teams spend 20 million.

The turbo power situation has got out of hand. So much attention and importance is placed on fast qualifying that they go out and blow up eight engines at £50,000 a time. I think we may yet have to go to something like the Indianapolis situation where they have a 'blow-off' valve, sealed by the scrutineers, which will 'go' on every car at the same pressure.

The television coverage of the sport is very good and whilst it continues the sponsors will always be forthcoming. Just imagine – 90 million people watching one race.

All of these aspects of Grand Prix racing are matters which in the next few years will require all the brilliance and shrewdness of Bernie Ecclestone if the sport is to continue to prosper. But however involved Bernie is in international affairs I have a sneaking suspicion that nothing will give him greater pleasure than to see more World Championship laurels won by a Brabham driver to add to those gained by Jack Brabham, Denny Hulme and Nelson Piquet.

The Brabham team is one of the most successful in motor-racing history. It is difficult to see anything changing that.

APPENDIX 1:

Brabham's World Championship Grand Prix Results 1962–84

Key: DNF: Did not Finish. DNQ: Did not Qualify. NC: Not Classified. DNS: Did not Start.
+ Subsequently disqualified. * Subsequently discounted as Championship round. ‡FOCA withdrew.

1962

German Grand Prix	Jack Brabham	Brabham-Climax BT3	DNF
United States Grand Prix	Jack Brabham	Brabham-Climax BT3	4th
South African Grand Prix	Jack Brabham	Brabham-Climax BT3	4th

World Championship position: Brabham (9th), 9 points.
Constructors' Cup: Brabham (7th), 9 points.

1963

Monaco Grand Prix	Dan Gurney	Brabham-Climax BT7	DNF
Belgian Grand Prix	Jack Brabham	Brabham-Climax BT3	DNF
	Dan Gurney	Brabham-Climax BT7	3rd
Dutch Grand Prix	Jack Brabham	Brabham-Climax BT7	DNF
	Dan Gurney	Brabham-Climax BT7	2nd
French Grand Prix	Jack Brabham	Brabham-Climax BT7	4th
	Dan Gurney	Brabham-Climax BT7	5th
British Grand Prix	Jack Brabham	Brabham-Climax BT7	DNF
	Dan Gurney	Brabham-Climax BT7	DNF
German Grand Prix	Jack Brabham	Brabham-Climax BT7	7th
	Dan Gurney	Brabham-Climax BT7	DNF
Italian Grand Prix	Jack Brabham	Brabham-Climax BT3	5th
	Dan Gurney	Brabham-Climax BT7	DNF
United States Grand Prix	Jack Brabham	Brabham-Climax BT7	4th
	Dan Gurney	Brabham-Climax BT7	DNF
Mexican Grand Prix	Jack Brabham	Brabham-Climax BT7	DNF
	Dan Gurney	Brabham-Climax BT7	2nd

World Championship positions: Gurney (5th), 19 points; Brabham (7th), 14 points.
Constructors' Cup: Brabham (3rd), 28 points.

1964

Monaco Grand Prix	Jack Brabham	Brabham-Climax BT7	DNF
	Dan Gurney	Brabham-Climax BT7	DNF
Dutch Grand Prix	Jack Brabham	Brabham-Climax BT7	DNF
	Dan Gurney	Brabham-Climax BT7	DNF
Belgian Grand Prix	Jack Brabham	Brabham-Climax BT7	3rd
	Dan Gurney	Brabham-Climax BT7	6th

Appendix 1

1964—*contd.*

French Grand Prix	Jack Brabham	Brabham-Climax BT7	3rd
	Dan Gurney	Brabham-Climax BT7	1st
British Grand Prix	Jack Brabham	Brabham-Climax BT7	4th
	Dan Gurney	Brabham-Climax BT7	13th
German Grand Prix	Jack Brabham	Brabham-Climax BT7	DNF
	Dan Gurney	Brabham-Climax BT7	10th
Austrian Grand Prix	Jack Brabham	Brabham-Climax BT11	9th
	Dan Gurney	Brabham-Climax BT7	DNF
Italian Grand Prix	Jack Brabham	Brabham-Climax BT11	DNF
	Dan Gurney	Brabham-Climax BT7	10th
United States Grand Prix	Jack Brabham	Brabham-Climax BT11	DNF
	Dan Gurney	Brabham-Climax BT7	DNF
Mexican Grand Prix	Jack Brabham	Brabham-Climax BT11	DNF
	Dan Gurney	Brabham-Climax BT7	1st

World Championship positions: Gurney (6th), 19 points; Brabham (8th), 11 points.
Constructors' Cup: Brabham (4th), 33 points.

1965

South African Grand Prix	Jack Brabham	Brabham-Climax BT11	8th
	Dan Gurney	Brabham-Climax BT11	DNF
Monaco Grand Prix	Jack Brabham	Brabham-Climax BT11	DNF
	Denny Hulme	Brabham-Climax BT7	8th
Belgian Grand Prix	Jack Brabham	Brabham-Climax BT11	4th
	Dan Gurney	Brabham-Climax BT11	10th
French Grand Prix	Dan Gurney	Brabham-Climax BT11	DNF
	Denny Hulme	Brabham-Climax BT11	4th
British Grand Prix	Jack Brabham	Brabham-Climax BT11	DNS
	Dan Gurney	Brabham-Climax BT11	6th
	Denny Hulme	Brabham-Climax BT7	DNF
Dutch Grand Prix	Dan Gurney	Brabham-Climax BT11	3rd
	Denny Hulme	Brabham-Climax BT11	8th
German Grand Prix	Jack Brabham	Brabham-Climax BT11	5th
	Dan Gurney	Brabham-Climax BT11	3rd
	Denny Hulme	Brabham-Climax BT7	DNF
Italian Grand Prix	Dan Gurney	Brabham-Climax BT11	3rd
	Denny Hulme	Brabham-Climax BT11	DNF
	Giancarlo Baghetti	Brabham-Climax BT7	DNF
United States Grand Prix	Jack Brabham	Brabham-Climax BT11	3rd
	Dan Gurney	Brabham-Climax BT11	2nd
Mexican Grand Prix	Jack Brabham	Brabham-Climax BT11	DNF
	Dan Gurney	Braham-Climax BT11	2nd

World Championship positions: Gurney (4th), 25 points; Brabham (10th), 9 points; Hulme (11th), 5 points.
Constructors' Cup: Brabham (3rd), 27 points.

1966

Monaco Grand Prix	Jack Brabham	Brabham-Repco BT19	DNF
	Denny Hulme	Brabham-Climax BT22	DNF

Belgian Grand Prix	Jack Brabham	Brabham-Repco BT22	4th
	Denny Hulme	Brabham-Climax BT22	DNF
French Grand Prix	Jack Brabham	Brabham-Repco BT19	1st
	Denny Hulme	Brabham-Repco BT20	3rd
British Grand Prix	Jack Brabham	Brabham-Repco BT 19	1st
	Denny Hulme	Brabham-Repco BT20	2nd
Dutch Grand Prix	Jack Brabham	Brabham-Repco BT 19	1st
	Denny Hulme	Brabham-Repco BT20	DNF
German Grand Prix	Jack Brabham	Brabham-Repco BT19	1st
	Denny Hulme	Brabham-Repco BT20	DNF
Italian Grand Prix	Jack Brabham	Brabham-Repco BT19	DNF
	Denny Hulme	Brabham-Repco BT20	3rd
United States Grand Prix	Jack Brabham	Brabham-Repco BT20	DNF
	Denny Hulme	Brabham-Repco BT20	DNF
Mexican Grand Prix	Jack Brabham	Brabham-Repco BT20	2nd
	Denny Hulme	Brabham-Repco BT20	3rd

World Championship positions: Brabham (1st), 42 points; Hulme (4th), 18 points.
Constructors' Cup: Brabham (1st), 42 points.

1967

South African Grand Prix	Jack Brabham	Brabham-Repco BT20	6th
	Denny Hulme	Brabham-Repco BT20	4th
Monaco Grand Prix	Jack Brabham	Brabham-Repco BT19	DNF
	Denny Hulme	Brabham-Repco BT20	1st
Dutch Grand Prix	Jack Brabham	Brabham-Repco BT19	2nd
	Denny Hulme	Brabham-Repco BT20	3rd
Belgian Grand Prix	Jack Brabham	Brabham-Repco BT24	DNF
	Denny Hulme	Brabham-Repco BT19	DNF
French Grand Prix	Jack Brabham	Brabham-Repco BT24	1st
	Denny Hulme	Brabham-Repco BT24	2nd
British Grand Prix	Jack Brabham	Brabham-Repco BT24	4th
	Denny Hulme	Brabham-Repco BT24	2nd
German Grand Prix	Jack Brabham	Brabham-Repco BT24	2nd
	Denny Hulme	Brabham-Repco BT24	1st
Canadian Grand Prix	Jack Brabham	Brabham-Repco BT24	1st
	Denny Hulme	Brabham-Repco BT24	2nd
Italian Grand Prix	Jack Brabham	Brabham-Repco BT24	2nd
	Denny Hulme	Brabham-Repco BT24	DNF
United States Grand Prix	Jack Brabham	Brabham-Repco BT24	5th
	Denny Hulme	Brabham-Repco BT24	3rd
Mexican Grand Prix	Jack Brabham	Brabham-Repco BT24	2nd
	Denny Hulme	Brabham-Repco BT24	3rd

World Championship positions: Hulme (1st) 51 points: Brabham (2nd) 46 points.
Constructors' Cup: Brabham (1st), 37 points.

1968

South African Grand Prix	Jack Brabham	Brabham-Repco BT24	DNF
	Jochen Rindt	Brabham-Repco BT24	3rd

1968—*contd.*

Spanish Grand Prix	Jack Brabham	Brabham-Repco BT26	DNS
	Jochen Rindt	Brabham-Repco BT24	DNF
Monaco Grand Prix	Jack Brabham	Brabham-Repco BT26	DNF
	Jochen Rindt	Brabham-Repco BT24	DNF
Belgian Grand Prix	Jack Brabham	Brabham-Repco BT26	DNF
	Jochen Rindt	Brabham-Repco BT26	DNF
Dutch Grand Prix	Jack Brabham	Brabham-Repco BT26	DNF
	Jochen Rindt	Brabham-Repco BT26	DNF
	Dan Gurney	Brabham-Repco BT24	DNF
French Grand Prix	Jack Brabham	Brabham-Repco BT26	DNF
	Jochen Rindt	Brabham-Repco BT26	DNF
British Grand Prix	Jack Brabham	Brabham-Repco BT26	DNF
	Jochen Rindt	Brabham-Repco BT26	DNF
German Grand Prix	Jack Brabham	Brabham-Repco BT26	5th
	Jochen Rindt	Brabham-Repco BT26	3rd
Italian Grand Prix	Jack Brabham	Brabham-Repco BT26	DNF
	Jochen Rindt	Brabham-Repco BT26	DNF
Canadian Grand Prix	Jack Brabham	Brabham-Repco BT26	DNF
	Jochen Rindt	Brabham-Repco BT26	DNF
United States Grand Prix	Jack Brabham	Brabham-Repco BT26	DNF
	Jochen Rindt	Brabham-Repco BT26	DNF
Mexican Grand Prix	Jack Brabham	Brabham-Repco BT26	10th
	Jochen Rindt	Brabham-Repco BT26	DNF

World Championship positions: Rindt (12th), 8 points; Brabham (23rd =), 2 points.
Constructors' Cup: Brabham (8th), 10 points.

1969

South African Grand Prix	Jack Brabham	Brabham-Cosworth BT26	DNF
	Jacky Ickx	Brabham-Cosworth BT26	DNF
Spanish Grand Prix	Jack Brabham	Brabham-Cosworth BT26	DNF
	Jacky Ickx	Brabham-Cosworth BT26	6th
Monaco Grand Prix	Jack Brabham	Brabham-Cosworth BT26	DNF
	Jacky Ickx	Brabham-Cosworth BT26	DNF
Dutch Grand Prix	Jack Brabham	Brabham-Cosworth BT26	6th
	Jacky Ickx	Brabham-Cosworth BT26	5th
French Grand Prix	Jacky Ickx	Brabham-Cosworth BT26A	3rd
British Grand Prix	Jacky Ickx	Brabham-Cosworth BT26A	2nd
German Grand Prix	Jacky Ickx	Brabham-Cosworth BT26A	1st
Italian Grand Prix	Jack Brabham	Brabham-Cosworth BT26A	DNF
	Jacky Ickx	Brabham-Cosworth BT26A	DNF
Canadian Grand Prix	Jack Brabham	Brabham-Cosworth BT26A	2nd
	Jacky Ickx	Brabham-Cosworth BT26A	1st
United States Grand Prix	Jack Brabham	Brabham-Cosworth BT26A	4th
	Jacky Ickx	Brabham-Cosworth BT26A	DNF
Mexican Grand Prix	Jack Brabham	Brabham-Cosworth BT26A	3rd
	Jacky Ickx	Brabham-Cosworth BT26A	2nd

World Championship positions: Ickx (2nd), 37 points; Brabham (10th), 14 points.
Constructors' Cup: Brabham (2nd), 51 points.

Appendix 1

1970

South African Grand Prix	Jack Brabham	Brabham-Cosworth BT33	1st
	Rolf Stommelen	Brabham-Cosworth BT33	DNF
Spanish Grand Prix	Jack Brabham	Brabham-Cosworth BT33	DNF
	Rolf Stommelen	Brabham-Cosworth BT33	DNF
Monaco Grand Prix	Jack Brabham	Brabham-Cosworth BT33	2nd
	Rolf Stommelen	Brabham-Cosworth BT33	DNQ
Belgian Grand Prix	Jack Brabham	Brabham-Cosworth BT33	DNF
	Rolf Stommelen	Brabham-Cosworth BT33	5th
Dutch Grand Prix	Jack Brabham	Brabham-Cosworth BT33	11th
	Rolf Stommelen	Brabham-Cosworth BT33	DNQ
French Grand Prix	Jack Brabham	Brabham-Cosworth BT33	3rd
	Rolf Stommelen	Brabham-Cosworth BT33	7th
British Grand Prix	Jack Brabham	Brabham-Cosworth BT33	2nd
	Rolf Stommelen	Brabham-Cosworth BT33	DNS
German Grand Prix	Jack Brabham	Brabham-Cosworth BT33	DNF
	Rolf Stommelen	Brabham-Cosworth BT33	5th
Austrian Grand Prix	Jack Brabham	Brabham-Cosworth BT33	13th
	Rolf Stommelen	Brabham-Cosworth BT33	3rd
Italian Grand Prix	Jack Brabham	Brabham-Cosworth BT33	DNF
	Rolf Stommelen	Brabham-Cosworth BT33	5th
Canadian Grand Prix	Jack Brabham	Brabham-Cosworth BT33	DNF
	Rolf Stommelen	Brabham-Cosworth BT33	DNF
United States Grand Prix	Jack Brabham	Brabham-Cosworth BT33	10th
	Rolf Stommelen	Brabham-Cosworth BT33	12th
Mexican Grand Prix	Jack Brabham	Brabham-Cosworth BT33	DNF
	Rolf Stommelen	Brabham-Cosworth BT33	DNF

World Championship positions: Brabham (5th =), 25 points; Stommelen (11th), 10 points.
Constructors' Cup: Brabham (4th =), 35 points.

1971

South African Grand Prix	Graham Hill	Brabham-Cosworth BT33	9th
	Dave Charlton	Brabham-Cosworth BT33	DNF
Spanish Grand Prix	Graham Hill	Brabham-Cosworth BT34	DNF
	Tim Schenken	Brabham-Cosworth BT33	9th
Monaco Grand Prix	Graham Hill	Brabham-Cosworth BT34	DNF
	Tim Schenken	Brabham-Cosworth BT33	9th
Dutch Grand Prix	Graham Hill	Brabham-Cosworth BT34	10th
	Tim Schenken	Brabham-Cosworth BT33	DNF
French Grand Prix	Graham Hill	Brabham-Cosworth BT34	DNF
	Tim Schenken	Brabham-Cosworth BT33	DNF
British Grand Prix	Graham Hill	Brabham-Cosworth BT34	DNF
	Tim Schenken	Brabham-Cosworth BT33	DNF
German Grand Prix	Graham Hill	Brabham-Cosworth BT34	9th
	Tim Schenken	Brabham-Cosworth BT33	6th
Austrian Grand Prix	Graham Hill	Brabham-Cosworth BT34	5th
	Tim Schenken	Brabham-Cosworth BT33	3rd
Italian Grand Prix	Graham Hill	Brabham-Cosworth BT34	DNF
	Tim Schenken	Brabham-Cosworth BT33	DNF

1971—*contd.*

Canadian Grand Prix	Graham Hill	Brabham-Cosworth BT34	DNF
	Tim Schenken	Brabham-Cosworth BT33	DNF
	Chris Craft	Brabham-Cosworth BT33	DNS
United States Grand Prix	Graham Hill	Brabham-Cosworth BT34	7th
	Tim Schenken	Brabham-Cosworth BT33	DNF
	Chris Craft	Brabham-Cosworth BT33	DNF

World *Championship positions:* Schenken (14th =), 5 points; Hill (21st), 2 points.
Constructors' Cup: Brabham (9th), 5 points.

1972

Argentine Grand Prix	Graham Hill	Brabham-Cosworth BT33	DNF
	Carlos Reutemann	Brabham-Cosworth BT34	7th '
South African Grand Prix	Graham Hill	Brabham-Cosworth BT33	6th
	Carlos Reutemann	Brabham-Cosworth BT34	DNF
Spanish Grand Prix	Graham Hill	Brabham-Cosworth BT37	10th
	Wilson Fittipaldi	Brabham-Cosworth BT33	7th
Monaco Grand Prix	Graham Hill	Brabham-Cosworth BT37	12th
	Wilson Fittipaldi	Brabham-Cosworth BT33	9th
Belgian Grand Prix	Graham Hill	Brabham-Cosworth BT37	DNF
	Carlos Reutemann	Brabham-Cosworth BT37	13th
	Wilson Fittipaldi	Brabham-Cosworth BT34	DNF
French Grand Prix	Graham Hill	Brabham-Cosworth BT37	10th
	Carlos Reutemann	Brabham-Cosworth BT37	12th
	Wilson Fittipaldi	Brabham-Cosworth BT34	8th
British Grand Prix	Graham Hill	Brabham-Cosworth BT37	DNF
	Carlos Reutemann	Brabham-Cosworth BT37	8th
	Wilson Fittipaldi	Brabham-Cosworth BT34	DNF
German Grand Prix	Graham Hill	Brabham-Cosworth BT37	6th
	Carlos Reutemann	Brabham-Cosworth BT37	DNF
	Wilson Fittipaldi	Brabham-Cosworth BT34	7th
Austrian Grand Prix	Graham Hill	Brabham-Cosworth BT37	DNF
	Carlos Reutemann	Brabham-Cosworth BT37	DNF
	Wilson Fittipaldi	Brabham-Cosworth BT34	DNF
Italian Grand Prix	Graham Hill	Brabham-Cosworth BT37	5th
	Carlos Reutemann	Brabham-Cosworth BT37	DNF
	Wilson Fittipaldi	Brabham-Cosworth BT34	DNF
Canadian Grand Prix	Graham Hill	Brabham-Cosworth BT37	8th
	Carlos Reutemann	Brabham-Cosworth BT34	4th
	Wilson Fittipaldi	Brabham-Cosworth BT34	DNF
United States Grand Prix	Graham Hill	Brabham-Cosworth BT37	11th
	Carlos Reutemann	Brabham-Cosworth BT37	DNF
	Wilson Fittipaldi	Brabham-Cosworth BT34	DNF

World Championship positions: Hill (12th =), 4 points; Reutemann (16th =), 3 points.
Constructors' Cup: Brabham, (9th), 7 points.

1973

Argentine Grand Prix	Carlos Reutemann	Brabham-Cosworth BT37	DNF
	Wilson Fittipaldi	Brabham-Cosworth BT37	6th
Brazilian Grand Prix	Carlos Reutemann	Brabham-Cosworth BT37	11th
	Wilson Fittipaldi	Brabham-Cosworth BT37	DNF

South African Grand Prix	Carlos Reutemann	Brabham-Cosworth BT37	7th
	Wilson Fittipaldi	Brabham-Cosworth BT37	DNF
Spanish Grand Prix	Carlos Reutemann	Brabham-Cosworth BT42	DNF
	Wilson Fittipaldi	Brabham-Cosworth BT42	10th
	Andrea de Adamich	Brabham-Cosworth BT37	DNF
Belgian Grand Prix	Carlos Reutemann	Brabham-Cosworth BT42	DNF
	Wilson Fittipaldi	Brabham-Cosworth BT42	DNF
	Andrea de Adamich	Brabham-Cosworth BT37	4th
Monaco Grand Prix	Carlos Reutemann	Brabham-Cosworth BT42	4th
	Wilson Fittipaldi	Brabham-Cosworth BT42	DNF
	Andrea de Adamich	Brabham-Cosworth BT37	7th
Swedish Grand Prix	Carlos Reutemann	Brabham-Cosworth BT42	4th
	Wilson Fittipaldi	Brabham-Cosworth BT42	DNF
French Grand Prix	Carlos Reutemann	Brabham-Cosworth BT42	3rd
	Wilson Fittipaldi	Brabham-Cosworth BT42	DNF
	Andrea de Adamich	Brabham-Cosworth BT37	DNF
British Grand Prix	Carlos Reutemann	Brabham-Cosworth BT42	6th
	Wilson Fittipaldi	Brabham-Cosworth BT42	DNF
	Andrea de Adamich	Brabham-Cosworth BT42	DNF
	John Watson	Brabham-Cosworth BT37	DNF
Dutch Grand Prix	Carlos Reutemann	Brabham-Cosworth BT42	DNF
	Wilson Fittipaldi	Brabham-Cosworth BT42	DNF
German Grand Prix	Carlos Reutemann	Brabham-Cosworth BT42	DNF
	Wilson Fittipaldi	Brabham-Cosworth BT42	5th
	Rolf Stommelen	Brabham-Cosworth BT42	11th
Italian Grand Prix	Carlos Reutemann	Brabham-Cosworth BT42	6th
	Wilson Fittipaldi	Brabham-Cosworth BT42	DNF
	Rolf Stommelen	Brabham-Cosworth BT42	12th
Canadian Grand Prix	Carlos Reutemann	Brabham-Cosworth BT42	8th
	Wilson Fittipaldi	Brabham-Cosworth BT42	11th
	Rolf Stommelen	Brabham-Cosworth BT42	12th
United States Grand Prix	Carlos Reutemann	Brabham-Cosworth BT42	3rd
	Wilson Fittipaldi	Brabham-Cosworth BT42	17th
	John Watson	Brabham-Cosworth BT42	DNF

World Championship positions: Reutemann (7th), 16 points; Fittipaldi and de Adamich (15th), 3 points
Constructors' Cup: Brabham (4th), 22 points.

1974

Argentine Grand Prix	Carlos Reutemann	Brabham-Cosworth BT44	7th
	Richard Robarts	Brabham-Cosworth BT44	DNF
Brazilian Grand Prix	Carlos Reutemann	Brabham-Cosworth BT44	7th
	Richard Robarts	Brabham-Cosworth BT44	15th
South African Grand Prix	Carlos Reutemann	Brabham-Cosworth BT44	1st
	Richard Robarts	Brabham-Cosworth BT44	17th
Spanish Grand Prix	Carlos Reutemann	Brabham-Cosworth BT44	DNF
	Rikki von Opel	Brabham-Cosworth BT44	DNF
Belgian Grand Prix	Carlos Reutemann	Brabham-Cosworth BT44	DNF
	Rikki von Opel	Brabham-Cosworth BT44	DNF
	Teddy Pilette	Brabham-Cosworth BT42	17th

1974—*contd.*

Monaco Grand Prix	Carlos Reutemann	Brabham-Cosworth BT44	DNF
	Rikki von Opel	Brabham-Cosworth BT44	DNQ
Swedish Grand Prix	Carlos Reutemann	Brabham-Cosworth BT44	DNF
	Rikki von Opel	Brabham-Cosworth BT44	9th
Dutch Grand Prix	Carlos Reutemann	Brabham-Cosworth BT44	12th
	Rikki von Opel	Brabham-Cosworth BT44	9th
French Grand Prix	Carlos Reutemann	Brabham-Cosworth BT44	DNF
	Rikki von Opel	Brabham-Cosworth BT44	DNQ
British Grand Prix	Carlos Reutemann	Brabham-Cosworth BT44	6th
	Carlos Pace	Brabham-Cosworth BT44	8th
German Grand Prix	Carlos Reutemann	Brabham-Cosworth BT44	3rd
	Carlos Pace	Brabham-Cosworth BT44	12th
Austrian Grand Prix	Carlos Reutemann	Brabham-Cosworth BT44	1st
	Carlos Pace	Brabham-Cosworth BT44	DNF
Italian Grand Prix	Carlos Reutemann	Brabham-Cosworth BT44	DNF
	Carlos Pace	Brabham-Cosworth BT44	5th
Canadian Grand Prix	Carlos Reutemann	Brabham-Cosworth BT44	9th
	Carlos Pace	Brabham-Cosworth BT44	8th
United States Grand Prix	Carlos Reutemann	Brabham-Cosworth BT44	1st
	Carlos Pace	Brabham-Cosworth BT44	2nd

World Championship positions: Reutemann (6th), 32 points; Pace (12th), 11 points.

1975

Argentine Grand Prix	Carlos Reutemann	Brabham-Cosworth BT44B	3rd
	Carlos Pace	Brabham-Cosworth BT44B	DNF
Brazilian Grand Prix	Carlos Reutemann	Brabham-Cosworth BT44B	8th
	Carlos Pace	Brabham-Cosworth BT44B	1st
South African Grand Prix	Carlos Reutemann	Brabham-Cosworth BT44B	2nd
	Carlos Pace	Brabham-Cosworth BT44B	4th
Spanish Grand Prix	Carlos Reutemann	Brabham-Cosworth BT44B	3rd
	Carlos Pace	Brabham-Cosworth BT44B	DNF
Monaco Grand Prix	Carlos Reutemann	Brabham-Cosworth BT44B	9th
	Carlos Pace	Brabham-Cosworth BT44B	3rd
Belgian Grand Prix	Carlos Reutemann	Brabham-Cosworth BT44B	3rd
	Carlos Pace	Brabham-Cosworth BT44B	8th
Swedish Grand Prix	Carlos Reutemann	Brabham-Cosworth BT44B	2nd
	Carlos Pace	Brabham-Cosworth BT44B	DNF
Dutch Grand Prix	Carlos Reutemann	Brabham-Cosworth BT44B	4th
	Carlos Pace	Brabham-Cosworth BT44B	5th
French Grand Prix	Carlos Reutemann	Brabham-Cosworth BT44B	14th
	Carlos Pace	Brabham-Cosworth BT44B	DNF
British Grand Prix	Carlos Reutemann	Brabham-Cosworth BT44B	DNF
	Carlos Pace	Brabham-Cosworth BT44B	2nd
German Grand Prix	Carlos Reutemann	Brabham-Cosworth BT44B	1st
	Carlos Pace	Brabham-Cosworth BT44B	DNF
Austrian Grand Prix	Carlos Reutemann	Brabham-Cosworth BT44B	14th
	Carlos Pace	Brabham-Cosworth BT44B	DNF
Italian Grand Prix	Carlos Reutemann	Brabham-Cosworth BT44B	4th
	Carlos Pace	Brabham-Cosworth BT44B	DNF

| United States Grand Prix | Carlos Reutemann | Brabham-Cosworth BT44B | DNF |
| | Carlos Pace | Brabham-Cosworth BT44B | DNF |

World Championship positions: Carlos Reutemann (3rd), 37 points; Carlos Pace (6th), 24 points.
Constructors' Cup: Brabham (2nd), 54 points.

1976

Brazilian Grand Prix	Carlos Reutemann	Brabham-Alfa Romeo BT45	12th
	Carlos Pace	Brabham-Alfa Romeo BT45	10th
South African Grand Prix	Carlos Reutemann	Brabham-Alfa Rpmeo BT45	DNF
	Carlos Pace	Brabham-Alfa Romeo BT45	DNF
United States Grand Prix West	Carlos Reutemann	Brabham-Alfa Romeo BT45	DNF
	Carlos Pace	Brabham-Alfa Romeo BT45	9th
Spanish Grand Prix	Carlos Reutemann	Brabham-Alfa Romeo BT45	4th
	Carlos Pace	Brabham-Alfa Romeo BT45	5th
Belgian Grand Prix	Carlos Reutemann	Brabham-Alfa Romeo BT45	DNF
	Carlos Pace	Brabham-Alfa Romeo BT45	DNF
Monaco Grand Prix	Carlos Reutemann	Brabham-Alfa Romeo BT45	DNF
	Carlos Pace	Brabham-Alfa Romeo BT45	9th
Swedish Grand Prix	Carlos Reutemann	Brabham-Alfa Romeo BT45	DNF
	Carlos Pace	Brabham-Alfa Romeo BT45	8th
French Grand Prix	Carlos Reutemann	Brabham-Alfa Romeo BT45	11th
	Carlos Pace	Brabham-Alfa Romeo BT45	4th
British Grand Prix	Carlos Reutemann	Brabham-Alfa Romeo BT45	DNF
	Carlos Pace	Brabham-Alfa Romeo BT45	8th
German Grand Prix	Carlos Reutemann	Brabham-Alfa Romeo BT45	DNF
	Carlos Pace	Brabham-Alfa Romeo BT45	4th
	Rolf Stommelen	Brabham-Alfa Romeo BT45	6th
Austrian Grand Prix	Carlos Reutemann	Brabham-Alfa Romeo BT45	DNF
	Carlos Pace	Brabham-Alfa Romeo BT45	DNF
Dutch Grand Prix	Carlos Reutemann	Brabham-Alfa Romeo BT45	DNF
	Carlos Pace	Brabham-Alfa Romeo BT45	DNF
Italian Grand Prix	Carlos Pace	Brabham-Alfa Romeo BT45	DNF
	Rolf Stommelen	Brabham-Alfa Romeo BT45	DNF
Canadian Grand Prix	Carlos Pace	Brabham-Alfa Romeo BT45	7th
	Larry Perkins	Brabham-Alfa Romeo BT45	17th
United States Grand Prix East	Carlos Pace	Brabham-Alfa Romeo BT45	DNF
	Larry Perkins	Brabham-Alfa Romeo BT45	DNF
Japanese Grand Prix	Carlos Pace	Brabham-Alfa Romeo BT45	DNF
	Larry Perkins	Brabham-Alfa Romeo BT45	DNF

World Championship positions: Pace (14th=), 7 points; Reutemann (16th=), 3 points.
Constructors' Cup: Brabham (9th), 9 points.

1977

Argentine Grand Prix	John Watson	Brabham-Alfa Romeo BT45	DNF
	Carlos Pace	Brabham-Alfa Romeo BT45	2nd
Brazilian Grand Prix	John Watson	Brabham-Alfa Romeo BT45	DNF
	Carlos Pace	Brabham-Alfa Romeo BT45	DNF
South African Grand Prix	John Watson	Brabham-Alfa Romeo BT45	6th
	Carlos Pace	Brabham-Alfa Romeo BT45B	13th

Appendix 1

1977—*contd.*

United States Grand Prix	John Watson	Brabham-Alfa Romeo BT45B	DNF
West	Hans Stuck	Brabham-Alfa Romeo BT45B	DNF
Spanish Grand Prix	John Watson	Brabham-Alfa Romeo BT45B	DNF
	Hans Stuck	Brabham-Alfa Romeo BT45B	6th
Monaco Grand Prix	John Watson	Brabham-Alfa Romeo BT45B	DNF
	Hans Stuck	Brabham-Alfa Romeo BT45B	DNF
Belgian Grand Prix	John Watson	Brabham-Alfa Romeo BT45B	DNF
	Hans Stuck	Brabham-Alfa Romeo BT45B	6th
Swedish Grand Prix	John Watson	Brabham-Alfa Romeo BT45B	5th
	Hans Stuck	Brabham-Alfa Romeo BT45B	10th
French Grand Prix	John Watson	Brabham-Alfa Romeo BT45B	2nd
	Hans Stuck	Brabham-Alfa Romeo BT45B	DNF
British Grand Prix	John Watson	Brabham-Alfa Romeo BT45B	DNF
	Hans Stuck	Brabham-Alfa Romeo BT45B	5th
German Grand Prix	John Watson	Brabham-Alfa Romeo BT45B	DNF
	Hans Stuck	Brabham-Alfa Romeo BT45B	3rd
Austrian Grand Prix	John Watson	Brabham-Alfa Romeo BT45B	8th
	Hans Stuck	Brabham-Alfa Romeo BT45B	3rd
Dutch Grand Prix	John Watson	Brabham-Alfa Romeo BT45B	DNF
	Hans Stuck	Brabham-Alfa Romeo BT45B	7th
Italian Grand Prix	John Watson	Brabham-Alfa Romeo BT45B	DNF
	Hans Stuck	Brabham-Alfa Romeo BT45B	DNF
	Giorgio Francia	Brabham-Alfa Romeo BT45B	DNQ
United States Grand Prix	John Watson	Brabham-Alfa Romeo BT45B	12th
East	Hans Stuck	Brabham-Alfa Romeo BT45B	DNF
Canadian Grand Prix	John Watson	Brabham-Alfa Romeo BT45B	DNF
	Hans Stuck	Brabham-Alfa Romeo BT45B	DNF
Japanese Grand Prix	John Watson	Brabham-Alfa Romeo BT45B	DNF
	Hans Stuck	Brabham-Alfa Romeo BT45B	7th

World Championship positions: Stuck (11th), 12 points; Watson (13th), 9 points; Pace (15th), 6 points.
Constructors' Cup: Brabham (5th), 27 points.

1978

Argentine Grand Prix	Niki Lauda	Brabham-Alfa Romeo BT45C	2nd
	John Watson	Brabham-Alfa Romeo BT45C	DNF
Brazilian Grand Prix	Niki Lauda	Brabham-Alfa Romeo BT45C	3rd
	John Watson	Brabham-Alfa Romeo BT45C	8th
South African Grand Prix	Niki Lauda	Brabham-Alfa Romeo BT46	DNF
	John Watson	Brabham-Alfa Romeo BT46	3rd
United States Grand Prix	Niki Lauda	Brabham-Alfa Romeo BT46	DNF
West	John Watson	Brabham-Alfa Romeo BT46	DNF
Monaco Grand Prix	Nlki Lauda	Brabham-Alfa Romeo BT46	2nd
	John Watson	Brabham-Alfa Romeo BT46	4th
Belgian Grand Prix	Niki Lauda	Brabham-Alfa Romeo BT46	DNF
	John Watson	Brabham-Alfa Romeo BT46	DNF
Spanish Grand Prix	Niki Lauda	Brabham-Alfa Romeo BT46	DNF
	John Watson	Brabham-Alfa Romeo BT46	5th
Swedish Grand Prix	Niki Lauda	Brabham-Alfa Romeo BT46	1st
	John Watson	Brabham-Alfa Romeo BT46	DNF

French Grand Prix	Niki Lauda	Brabham-Alfa Romeo BT46	DNF
	John Watson	Brabham-Alfa Romeo BT46	4th
British Grand Prix	Niki Lauda	Brabham-Alfa Romeo BT46	2nd
	John Watson	Brabham-Alfa Romeo BT46	3rd
German Grand Prix	Niki Lauda	Brabham-Alfa Romeo BT46	DNF
	John Watson	Brabham-Alfa Romeo BT46	7th
Austrian Grand Prix	Niki Lauda	Brabham-Alfa Romeo BT46	DNF
	John Watson	Brabham-Alfa Romeo BT46	7th
Dutch Grand Prix	Niki Lauda	Brabham-Alfa Romeo BT46	3rd
	John Watson	Brabham-Alfa Romeo BT46	4th
Italian Grand Prix	Niki Lauda	Brabham-Alfa Romeo BT46	1st
	John Watson	Brabham-Alfa Romeo BT46	2nd
United States Grand Prix	Niki Lauda	Brabham-Alfa Romeo BT46	DNF
East	John Watson	Brabham-Alfa Romeo BT46	DNF
Canadian Grand Prix	Niki Lauda	Brabham-Alfa Romeo BT46	DNF
	John Watson	Brabham-Alfa Romeo BT46	DNF
	Nelson Piquet	Brabham-Alfa Romeo BT46	11th

World Championship positions: Lauda (4th), 44 points; Watson (6th), 25 points.
Constructors' Cup: Brabham (3rd), 53 points.

1979

Argentine Grand Prix	Niki Lauda	Brabham-Alfa Romeo BT48	DNF
	Nelson Piquet	Brabham-Alfa Romeo BT46	DNF
Brazilian Grand Prix	Niki Lauda	Brabham-Alfa Romeo BT48	DNF
	Nelson Piquet	Brabham-Alfa Romeo BT48	DNF
South African Grand Prix	Niki Lauda	Brabham-Alfa Romeo BT48	6th
	Nelson Piquet	Brabham-Alfa Romeo BT48	7th
United States Grand Prix	Niki Lauda	Brabham-Alfa Romeo BT48	DNF
West	Nelson Piquet	Brabham-Alfa Romeo BT48	8th
Spanish Grand Prix	Niki Lauda	Brabham-Alfa Romeo BT48	DNF
	Nelson Piquet	Brabham-Alfa Romeo BT48	DNF
Belgian Grand Prix	Niki Lauda	Brabham-Alfa Romeo BT48	DNF
	Nelson Piquet	Brabham-Alfa Romeo BT48	DNF
Monaco Grand Prix	Niki Lauda	Brabham-Alfa Romeo BT48	DNF
	Nelson Piquet	Brabham-Alfa Romeo BT48	DNF
French Grand Prix	Niki Lauda	Brabham-Alfa Romeo BT48	DNF
	Nelson Piquet	Brabham-Alfa Romeo BT48	DNF
British Grand Prix	Niki Lauda	Brabham-Alfa Romeo BT48	DNF
	Nelson Piquet	Brabham-Alfa Romeo BT48	DNF
German Grand Prix	Niki Lauda	Brabham-Alfa Romeo BT48	DNF
	Nelson Piquet	Brabham-Alfa Romeo BT48	12th
Austrian Grand Prix	Niki Lauda	Brabham-Alfa Romeo BT48	DNF
	Nelson Piquet	Brabham-Alfa Romeo BT48	DNF
Dutch Grand Prix	Niki Lauda	Brabham-Alfa Romeo BT48	DNF
	Nelson Piquet	Brabham-Alfa Romeo BT48	4th
Italian Grand Prix	Niki Lauda	Brabham-Alfa Romeo BT48	4th
	Nelson Piquet	Brabham-Alfa Romeo BT48	DNF

1979—*contd.*

Canadian Grand Prix	Niki Lauda	Brabham-Cosworth BT49	DNS
	Nelson Piquet	Brabham-Cosworth BT49	DNF
	Ricardo Zunino	Brabham-Cosworth BT49	7th
United States Grand Prix	Nelson Piquet	Brabham-Cosworth BT49	DNF
East	Ricardo Zunino	Brabham-Cosworth BT49	DNF

World Championship positions: Lauda (14th), 4 points; Piquet (15th=), 3 points.
Constructors' Cup: Brabham (8th), 6 points.

1980

Argentine Grand Prix	Nelson Piquet	Brabham-Cosworth BT49	2nd
	Ricardo Zunino	Brabham-Cosworth BT49	7th
Brazilian Grand Prix	Nelson Piquet	Brabham-Cosworth BT49	DNF
	Ricardo Zunino	Brabham-Cosworth BT49	8th
South African Grand Prix	Nelson Piquet	Brabham-Cosworth BT49	4th
	Ricardo Zunino	Brabham-Cosworth BT49	10th
United States Grand Prix	Nelson Piquet	Brabham-Cosworth BT49	1st
West	Ricardo Zunino	Brabham-Cosworth BT49	DNF
Belgian Grand Prix	Nelson Piquet	Brabham-Cosworth BT49	DNF
	Ricardo Zunino	Brabham-Cosworth BT49	DNF
Monaco Grand Prix	Nelson Piquet	Brabham-Cosworth BT49	3rd
	Ricardo Zunino	Brabham-Cosworth BT49	DNQ
Spanish Grand Prix	Nelson Piquet	Brabham-Cosworth BT49	DNF
	Ricardo Zunino	Brabham-Cosworth BT49	DNF
French Grand Prix	Nelson Piquet	Brabham-Cosworth BT49	4th
	Ricardo Zunino	Brabham-Cosworth BT49	DNF
British Grand Prix	Nelson Piquet	Brabham-Cosworth BT49	2nd
	Hector Rebaque	Brabham-Cosworth BT49	7th
German Grand Prix	Nelson Piquet	Brabham-Cosworth BT49	4th
	Hector Rebaque	Brabham-Cosworth BT49B	DNF
Austrian Grand Prix	Nelson Piquet	Brabham-Cosworth BT49	5th
	Hector Rebaque	Brabham-Cosworth BT49B	10th
Dutch Grand Prix	Nelson Piquet	Brabham-Cosworth BT49	1st
	Hector Rebaque	Brabham-Cosworth BT49B	DNF
Italian Grand Prix	Nelson Piquet	Brabham-Cosworth BT49	1st
	Hector Rebaque	Brabham-Cosworth BT49	DNF
Canadian Grand Prix	Nelson Piquet	Brabham-Cosworth BT49	DNF
	Hector Rebaque	Brabham-Cosworth BT49	6th
United States Grand Prix	Nelson Piquet	Brabham-Cosworth BT49	DNF
East	Hector Rebaque	Brabham-Cosworth BT49	DNF

World Championship positions: Piquet (2nd), 54 points; Rebaque (20th=), 1 point.
Constructors' Cup: Brabham (3rd), 55 points.

1981

South African Grand Prix	Nelson Piquet	Brabham-Cosworth BT49	2nd
	Ricardo Zunino	Brabham-Cosworth BT49B	8th
United States Grand Prix	Nelson Piquet	Brabham-Cosworth BT49C	3rd
West	Hestor Rebaque	Brabham-Cosworth BT49C	DNF
Brazilian Grand Prix	Nelson Piquet	Brabham-Cosworth BT49C	12th
	Hector Rebaque	Brabham-Cosworth BT49C	DNF

Argentine Grand Prix	Nelson Piquet	Brabham-Cosworth BT49C	1st
	Hector Rabaque	Brabham-Cosworth BT49C	DNF
San Marino Grand Prix	Nelson Piquet	Brabham-Cosworth BT49C	1st
	Hector Rebaque	Brabham-Cosworth BT49C	4th
Belgian Grand Prix	Nelson Piquet	Brabham-Cosworth BT49C	DNF
	Hector Rebaque	Brabham-Cosworth BT49C	DNF
Monaco Grand Prix	Nelson Piquet	Brabham-Cosworth BT49C	DNF
	Hector Rebaque	Brabham-Cosworth BT49C	DNQ
Spanish Grand Prix	Nelson Piquet	Brabham-Cosworth BT49C	DNF
	Hector Rebaque	Brabham-Cosworth BT49C	DNF
French Grand Prix	Nelson Piquet	Brabham-Cosworth BT49C	3rd
	Hector Rebaque	Brabham-Coswoirth BT49C	9th
British Grand Prix	Nelson Piquet	Brabham-Cosworth BT49C	DNF
	Hector Rebaque	Brabham-Cosworth BT49C	5th
German Grand Prix	Nelson Piquet	Brabham-Cosworth BT49C	1st
	Hector Rebaque	Brabham-Cosworth BT49C	4th
Austrian Grand Prix	Nelson Piquet	Brabham-Cosworth BT49C	3rd
	Hector Rebaque	Brabham-Cosworth BT49C	DNF
Dutch Grand Prix	Nelson Piquet	Brabham-Cosworth BT49C	2nd
	Hector Rebaque	Brabham-Cosworth BT49C	4th
Italian Grand Prix	Nelson Piquet	Brabham-Cosworth BT49C	6th
	Hector Rebaque	Brabham-Cosworth BT49C	DNF
Canadian Grand Prix	Nelson Piquet	Brabham-Cosworth BT49C	5th
	Hector Rebaque	Brabham-Cosworth BT49C	DNF
Caesar's Palace Grand Prix	Nelson Piquet	Brabham-Cosworth BT49C	5th
	Hector Rebaque	Brabham-Cosworth BT49C	DNF

World Championship positions: Piquet (1st), 50 points; Rebaque (9th =), 11 points.
Constructors' Cup: Brabham (2nd), 61 points.

1982

South African Grand Prix	Nelson Piquet	Brabham-BMW BT50	DNF
	Riccardo Patrese	Brabham-BMW BT50	DNF
Brazilian Grand Prix	Nelson Piquet	Brabham-Cosworth BT49D	1st +
	Riccardo Patrese	Brabham-Cosworth BT49D	DNF
United States Grand Prix West	Nelson Piquet	Brabham-Cosworth BT49D	DNF
	Riccardo Patrese	Brabham-Cosworth BT49D	3rd
San Marino Grand Prix	Nelson Piquet		DNS†
	Riccardo Patrese		DNS†
Belgian Grand Prix	Nelson Piquet	Brabham-BMW BT50	5th
	Riccardo Patrese	Brabham-BMW BT50	DNF
Monaco Grand Prix	Nelson Piquet	Brabham-BMW BT 50	DNF
	Riccardo Patrese	Brabham-Cosworth BT49D	1st
USA East Grand Prix	Nelson Piquet	Brabham-BMW BT50	DNQ
	Riccardo Patrese	Brabham-Cosworth BT49D	DNF
Canadian Grand Prix	Nelson Piquet	Brabham-BMW BT50	1st
	Riccardo Patrese	Brabham-Cosworth BT49D	2nd
Dutch Grand Prix	Nelson Piquet	Brabham-BMW BT50	2nd
	Riccard Patrese	Brabham-BMW BT50	15th
British Grand Prix	Nelson Piquet	Brabham-BMW BT50	DNF
	Riccardo Patrese	Brabham-BMW BT50	DNF

1982—*contd.*

French Grand Prix	Nelson Piquet	Brabham-BMW BT50	DNF
	Riccardo Patrese	Brabham-BMW BT50	DNF
German Grand Prix	Nelson Piquet	Brabham-BMW BT50	DNF
	Ricardo Patrese	Brabham-BMW BT50	DNF
Austrian Grand Prix	Nelson Piquet	Brabham-BMW BT50	DNF
	Ricardo Patrese	Brabham-BMW BT50	DNF
Switzerland Grand Prix	Nelson Piquet	Brabham-BMW BT50	4th
	Ricardo Patrese	Brabham-BMW BT50	5th
Italian Grand Prix	Nelson Piquet	Brabham-BMW BT50	DNF
	Ricardo Patrese	Brabham-BMW BT50	DNF
USA Grand Prix	Nelson Piquet	Brabham-BMW BT50	DNF
	Ricardo Patrese	Brabham-BMW BT50	DNF

World Championship positions: Piquet (11th), 20 points; Patrese (10th), 21 points
Constructors' Cup: Brabham (5th) 41 points.

1983

Brazilian Grand Prix	Nelson Piquet	Brabham-BMW BT 52	1st
	Ricardo Patrese	Brabham-BMW BT52	DNF
USA West Grand Prix	Nelson Piquet	Brabham-BMW BT52	DNF
	Ricardo Patrese	Brabham-BMW BT52	10th
French Grand Prix	Nelson Piquet	Brabham-BMW BT52	2nd
	Ricardo Patrese	Brabham-BMW BT52	DNF
San Marino Grand Prix	Nelson Piquet	Brabham-BMW BT52	DNF
	Ricardo Patrese	Brabham-BMW BT52	DNF
Monaco Grand Prix	Nelson Piquet	Brabham-BMW BT52	2nd
	Ricardo Patrese	Brabham-BMW BT52	DNF
Belgian Grand Prix	Nelson Piquet	Brabham-BMW BT52	4th
	Ricardo Patrese	Brabham-BMW BT52	DNF
USA East Grand Prix	Nelson Piquet	Brabham-BMW BT52	4th
	Ricardo Patrese	Brabham-BMW BT52	DNF
Canadian Grand Prix	Nelson Piquet	Brabham-BMW BT52	DNF
	Ricardo Patrese	Brabham-BMW BT52	DNF
British Grand Prix	Nelson Piquet	Brabham-BMW BT52B	2nd
	Ricardo Patrese	Brabham-BMW BT52B	DNF
German Grand Prix	Nelson Piquet	Brabham-BMW BT52B	13th
	Ricardo Patrese	Brabham-BMW BT52B	3rd
Austrian Grand Prix	Nelson Piquet	Brabham-BMW BT52B	3rd
	Ricardo Patrese	Brabham-BMW BT52B	DNF
Dutch Grand Prix	Nelson Piquet	Brabham-BMW BT52B	DNF
	Ricardo Patrese	Brabham-BMW BT52B	9th
Italian Grand Prix	Nelson Piquet	Brabham-BMW BT52B	1st
	Ricardo Patrese	Brabham-BMW BT52B	DNF
European Grand Prix	Nelson Piquet	Brabham-BMW BT52B	1st
(Brands Hatch)	Ricardo Patrese	Brabham-BMW BT52B	7th
South African Grand Prix	Nelson Piquet	Brabham-BMW BT52B	3rd
	Ricardo Patrese	Brabham-BMW BT52B	1st

World Championship positions: Piquet (1st), 59 points; Patrese, (9th), 13 points.
Constructors' Cup: Brabham (3rd) 72 points.

1984

Brazilian Grand Prix	Nelson Piquet	Brabham-BMW BT53 Turbo	DNF
	Teo Fabi	Brabham-BMW BT53 Turbo	DNF
South African Grand Prix	Nelson Piquet	Brabham-BMW BT53 Turbo	DNF
	Teo Fabi	Brabham-BMW BT53 Turbo	DNF
Belgian Grand Prix	Nelson Piquet	Brabham-BMW BT53 Turbo	10th
	Teo Fabi	Brabham-BMW BT53 Turbo	DNF
San Marino Grand Prix	Nelson Piquet	Brabham-BMW BT53 Turbo	DNF
	Teo Fabi	Brabham-BMW BT53 Turbo	DNF
French Grand Prix	Nelson Piquet	Brabham-BMW BT53 Turbo	DNF
	Teo Fabi	Brabham-BMW BT53 Turbo	9th
Monaco Grand Prix	Nelson Piquet	Brabham-BMW BT53 Turbo	DNF
	Corrado Fabi	Brabham-BMW BT53 Turbo	DNF
Canadian Grand Prix	Nelson Piquet	Brabham-BMW BT53 Turbo	1st
	Corrado Fabi	Brabham-BMW BT53 Turbo	DNF
USA East Grand Prix	Nelson Piquet	Brabham-BMW BT53 Turbo	1st
(Detroit)	Teo Fabi	Brabham-BMW BT53 Turbo	4th
USA Dallas	Nelson Piquet	Brabham-BMW BT53 Turbo	DNF
	Corrado Fabi	Brabham-BMW BT53 Turbo	7th
British Grand Prix	Nelson Piquet	Brabham-BMW BT53 Turbo	7th
	Teo Fabi	Brabham-BMW BT53 Turbo	DNF
German Grand Prix	Nelson Piquet	Brabham-BMW BT53 Turbo	DNF
	Teo Fabi	Brabham-BMW BT53 Turbo	DNF
Austrian Grand Prix	Nelson Piquet	Brabham-BMW BT53 Turbo	2nd
	Teo Fabi	Brabham-BMW BT53 Turbo	4th
Dutch Grand Prix	Nelson Piquet	Brabham-BMW BT53 Turbo	DNF
	Teo Fabi	Brabham-BMW BT53 Turbo	5th
Italian Grand Prix	Nelson Piquet	Brabham-BMW BT53 Turbo	DNF
	Teo Fabi	Brabham-BMW BT53 Turbo	DNF
European Grand Prix	Nelson Piquet	Brabham-BMW BT53 Turbo	3rd
(Nürburgring)	Teo Fabi	Brabham-BMW BT53 Turbo	DNF
Portuguese Grand Prix	Nelson Piquet	Brabham-BMW BT53 Turbo	6th
	Manfred Winkelhock	Brabham-BMW BT53 Turbo	10th

World Championship positions: Piquet (5th), 29 points; Teo Fabi 8 points; Winkelhock 1 point.
Constructors' Cup: Brabham (4th), 38 points.

APPENDIX 2:

Brabham's Indianapolis 500 Results 1964-72

Key: DNF: Did not Finish. DNQ: Did not Qualify.

1964
Jack Brabham   Brabham-Offenhauser   20th

1965
Mario Andretti   Brabham-Ford   3rd
Jim McElreath   Brabham-Ford   20th

1966
Jim McElreath   Brabham-Ford   3rd

1967
Jim McElreath   Brabham-Ford   5th
Mario Andretti   Brabham-Ford   30th

1968
Jochen Rindt   Brabham-Repco   DNF
Bruce Walkup   Brabham-Offenhauser   DNQ

1969
Peter Revson   Brabham-Repco   5th
Sonny Ales   Brabham-Offenhauser   17th
Jack Brabham   Brabham-Repco   24th

1970
Jack Brabham   Brabham-Repco   13th
Bill Vukovich   Brabham-Offenhauser   25th

1971
Bill Vukovich   Brabham-Offenhauser   5th
Bud Tingelstad   Brabham-Offenhauser   7th

1972
John Martin   Brabham-Offenhauser   16th
Johnny Rutherford   Brabham-Offenhauser   27th

INDEX

183